CAMBRIDGE
UNIVERSITY PRESS

Chemistry

for Cambridge IGCSE™

EXAM PREPARATION AND PRACTICE

Margaret Mary McFadyen, Onn May Ling & Mei Qi Chew

Contents

Practical past-paper practice

An additional Practical guidance chapter and some digital questions can be found online at Cambridge GO.
For more information on how to access and use your digital resource, please see inside front cover.

> How to use this series

This suite of resources supports students and teachers following the Cambridge IGCSE™ Chemistry syllabus (0620). All of the components in the series are designed to work together and help students develop the necessary knowledge and skills for this subject. With clear language and style, they are designed for international students.

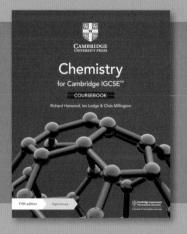

The coursebook provides coverage of the full Cambridge IGCSE Chemistry syllabus (0620). Each chapter explains facts and concepts, and uses relevant real-world examples of scientific principles to bring the subject to life. Together with a focus on practical work and plenty of active learning opportunities, the coursebook prepares learners for all aspects of their scientific study. Questions and exam-style questions in every chapter help learners to consolidate their understanding and provide practice opportunities to apply their learning.

The teacher's resource contains detailed guidance for all topics of the syllabus, including common misconceptions, identifying areas where learners might need extra support, as well as an engaging bank of lesson ideas for each syllabus topic. Differentiation is emphasised with suggestions of appropriate interventions to support and stretch learners. It also contains support for preparing and carrying out all the investigations in the practical workbook, including a set of sample results for when practicals aren't possible. Also included are scaffolded worksheets and unit tests for each chapter, as well as answers to all questions in every resource across this series.

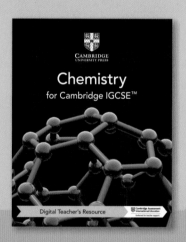

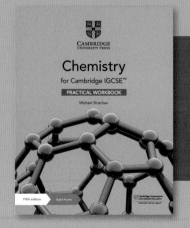

This workbook provides learners with additional opportunities for hands-on practical work, giving them full guidance and support that will help them to develop their investigative skills. These skills include planning investigations, selecting and handling apparatus, creating hypotheses, recording and displaying results, and analysing and evaluating data.

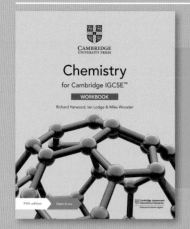

The skills-focused workbook has been constructed to help learners develop the skills that they need as they progress through their Cambridge IGCSE Chemistry course, providing practice of all the topics in the coursebook. A three-tier, scaffolded approach to skills development enables students to progress through 'focus', 'practice' and 'challenge' exercises, ensuring that every learner is supported.

Our research shows that English language skills are the single biggest barrier to students accessing international science. This write-in workbook contains exercises set within the context of IGCSE Chemistry topics to consolidate understanding and embed practice in aspects of language central to the subject.

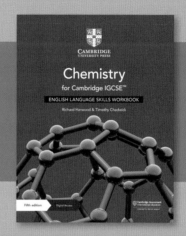

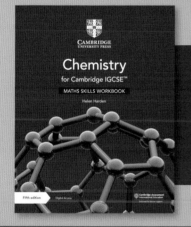

Mathematics is an integral part of scientific study, and one that learners often find a barrier to progression in science. The Maths Skills for Cambridge IGCSE Chemistry write-in workbook has been written in collaboration with the Association of Science Education, with each chapter focusing on several maths skills that their research concluded that students need to succeed in their Chemistry course.

The Exam Preparation and Practice resource provides dedicated support for learners in preparing for their final assessments. Hundreds of questions in the book and accompanying digital resource will help learners to check that they understand, and can recall, syllabus concepts. To help learners to show what they know in an exam context, a checklist of exam skills with corresponding questions, and past paper question practice, is also included. Self-assessment and reflection features support learners to identify any areas that need further practice. This resource should be used alongside the coursebook, throughout the course of study, so learners can most effectively increase their confidence and readiness for their exams.

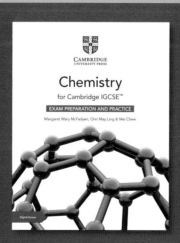

〉 How to use this book

This book will help you to check that you **know** the content of the syllabus and practise how to **show** this understanding in an exam. It will also help you be cognitively prepared and in the **flow**, ready for your exam. Research has shown that it is important that you do all three of these things, so we have designed the Know, Show, Flow approach to help you prepare effectively for exams.

Know — You will need to consolidate and then recall a lot of syllabus content.

Show — You should demonstrate your knowledge in the context of a Cambridge exam.

Flow — You should be cognitively engaged and ready to learn. This means reducing test anxiety.

Exam skills checklist

Category	Exam skill
Understanding the question	Recognise different question types
	Understand command words
	Mark scheme awareness
Providing an appropriate response	Understand connections between concepts
	Keep to time
	Know what a good answer looks like
Developing supportive behaviours	Reflect on progress
	Manage test anxiety

This **Exam skills checklist** helps you to develop the awareness, behaviours and habits that will support you when revising and preparing for your exams. For more exam skills advice, including understanding command words and managing your time effectively, please go to the **Exam skills chapter**.

Know

The full syllabus content of your IGCSE Chemistry course is covered in your Cambridge coursebook. This book will provide you with different types of questions to support you as you prepare for your exams. You will answer **Knowledge recall questions** that are designed to make sure you understand a topic, and **Recall and connect questions** to help you recall past learning and connect different concepts.

KNOWLEDGE FOCUS

Knowledge focus boxes summarise the topics that you will answer questions on in each chapter of this book. You can refer back to your Cambridge coursebook to remind yourself of the full detail of the syllabus content.

You will find **Knowledge recall questions** to make sure you understand a topic, and **Recall and connect questions** to help you recall past learning and connect different concepts. It is recommended that you answer the Knowledge recall questions just after you have covered the relevant topic in class, and then return to them at a later point to check you have properly understood the content.

Knowledge recall question

Testing yourself is a good way to check that your understanding is secure. These questions will help you to recall the core knowledge you have acquired during your course, and highlight any areas where you may need more practice. They are indicated with a blue bar with a gap, at the side of the page. We recommend that you answer the Knowledge recall questions just after you have covered the relevant topic in class, and then return to them at a later point to check you have properly understood the content.

⟪ RECALL AND CONNECT ⟪

To consolidate your learning, you need to test your memory frequently. These questions will test that you remember what you learned in previous chapters, in addition to what you are practising in the current chapter.

UNDERSTAND THESE TERMS

These list the important vocabulary that you should understand for each chapter. Definitions are provided in the glossary of your Cambridge coursebook.

Show

Exam questions test specific knowledge, skills and understanding. You need to be prepared so that you have the best opportunity to show what you know in the time you have during the exam. In addition to practising recall of the syllabus content, it is important to build your exam skills throughout the year.

EXAM SKILLS FOCUS

This feature outlines the exam skills you will practise in each chapter, alongside the Knowledge focus. They are drawn from the core set of eight exam skills, listed in the exam skills checklist. You will practise specific exam skills, such as understanding command words, within each chapter. More general exam skills, such as managing text anxiety, are covered in the Exam skills chapter.

Exam skills question

These questions will help you to develop your exam skills and demonstrate your understanding. To help you become familiar with exam-style questioning, these questions follow the style and use the language of real exam questions, and have allocated marks. They are indicated with a solid red bar at the side of the page.

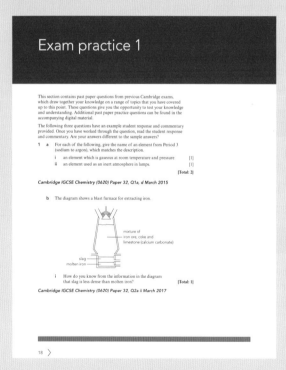

Looking at sample answers to past paper questions helps you to understand what to aim for.

The **Exam practice** sections in this resource contain example student responses and examiner-style commentary showing how the answer could be improved (both written by the authors).

Flow

Preparing for exams can be stressful. One of the approaches recommended by educational psychologists to help with this stress is to improve behaviours around exam preparation. This involves testing yourself in manageable chunks, accompanied by self-evaluation. You should avoid cramming, and build in more preparation time. This book is structured to help you do this.

Increasing your ability to recognise the signs of exam-related stress and working through some techniques for how to cope with it will help to make your exam preparation manageable.

REFLECTION

This feature asks you to think about the approach that you take to your exam preparation, and how you might improve this in the future. Reflecting on how you plan, monitor and evaluate your revision and preparation will help you to do your best in your exams.

SELF-ASSESSMENT CHECKLIST

These checklists return to the Learning intentions from your coursebook, as well as the Exam skills focus boxes from each chapter. Checking in on how confident you feel in each of these areas will help you to focus your exam preparation. The 'Show it' prompts will allow you to test your rating. You should revisit any areas that you rate 'Needs more work' or 'Almost there'.

Now I can:	Show it	Needs more work	Almost there	Confident to move on

Increasing your ability to recognise the signs of exam-related stress and working through some techniques for how to cope with it will help to make your exam preparation manageable. The **Exam skills chapter** will support you with this.

Digital support

Extra self-assessment questions for all chapters can be found online at Cambridge GO. For more information on how to access and use your digital resource, please see inside the front cover.

You will find **Answers** for all of the questions in the book on the 'supporting resources' area of the Cambridge GO platform.

Multiple choice questions

These ask you to select the correct answer to a question from four options. These are auto-marked and feedback is provided.

Flip card questions

These present a question on one screen, and suggested answers on the reverse.

Syllabus assessment objectives for IGCSE Chemistry

You should be familiar with the Assessment Objectives from the syllabus, as you will need to show evidence of these requirements in your responses.

The assessment objectives for this syllabus are:

Assessment objective	IGCSE weighting
AO1: Knowledge with understanding	50%
AO2: Handling information and problem-solving	30%
AO3: Experimental skills and investigations	20%

Exam skills

by Lucy Parsons

What's the point of this book?

Most students make one really basic mistake when they're preparing for exams. What is it? It's focusing far too much on learning 'stuff' – that's facts, figures, ideas, information – and not nearly enough time practising exam skills.

The students who work really, really hard but are disappointed with their results are nearly always students who focus on memorising stuff. They think to themselves, 'I'll do practice papers once I've revised everything.' The trouble is, they start doing practice papers too late to really develop and improve how they communicate what they know.

What could they do differently?

When your final exam script is assessed, it should contain specific language, information and thinking skills in your answers. If you read a question in an exam and you have no idea what you need to do to give a good answer, the likelihood is that your answer won't be as brilliant as it could be. That means your grade won't reflect the hard work you've put into revising for the exam.

There are different types of questions used in exams to assess different skills. You need to know how to recognise these question types and understand what you need to show in your answers.

So, how do you understand what to do in each question type?

That's what this book is all about. But first a little background.

Meet Benjamin Bloom

The psychologist Benjamin Bloom developed a way of classifying and valuing different skills we use when we learn, such as analysis and recalling information. We call these thinking skills. It's known as Bloom's Taxonomy and it's what most exam questions are based around.

If you understand Bloom's Taxonomy, you can understand what any type of question requires you to do. So, what does it look like?

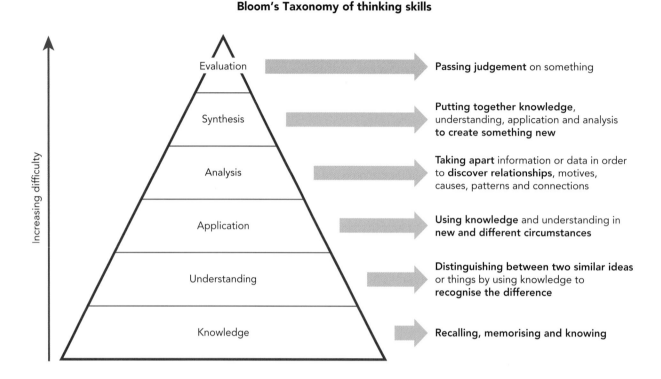

Bloom's Taxonomy of thinking skills

The key things to take away from this diagram are:

- Knowledge and understanding are known as lower-level thinking skills. They are less difficult than the other thinking skills. Exam questions that just test you on what you know are usually worth the lowest number of marks.

- All the other thinking skills are worth higher numbers of marks in exam questions. These questions need you to have some foundational knowledge and understanding but are far more about how you think than what you know. They involve:

  - Taking what you know and using it in unfamiliar situations (application).

  - Going deeper into information to discover relationships, motives, causes, patterns and connections (analysis).

  - Using what you know and think to create something new – whether that's an essay, long-answer exam question a solution to a maths problem, or a piece of art (synthesis).

  - Assessing the value of something, e.g. the reliability of the results of a scientific experiment (evaluation).

In this introductory chapter, you'll be shown how to develop the skills that enable you to communicate what you know and how you think. This will help you achieve to the best of your abilities. In the rest of the book, you'll have a chance to practise these exam skills by understanding how questions work and understanding what you need to show in your answers.

Every time you pick up this book and do a few questions, you're getting closer to achieving your dream results. So, let's get started!

Exam preparation and revision skills

What is revision?

If you think about it, the word 'revision' has two parts to it:

- re – which means 'again'

- vision – which is about seeing.

So, revision is literally about 'seeing again'. This means you're looking at something that you've already learned.

Typically, a teacher will teach you something in class. You may then do some questions on it, write about it in some way, or even do a presentation. You might then have an end-of-topic test sometime later. To prepare for this test, you need to 'look again' or revise what you were originally taught.

Step 1: Making knowledge stick

Every time you come back to something you've learned or revised you're improving your understanding and memory of that particular piece of knowledge. This is called **spaced retrieval**. This is how human memory works. If you don't use a piece of knowledge by recalling it, you lose it.

Everything we learn has to be physically stored in our brains by creating neural connections – joining brain cells together. The more often we 'retrieve' or recall a particular piece of knowledge, the stronger the neural connection gets. It's like lifting weights – the more often you lift, the stronger you get.

However, if you don't use a piece of knowledge for a long time, your brain wants to recycle the brain cells and use them for another purpose. The neural connections get weaker until they finally break, and the memory has gone. This is why it's really important to return often to things that you've learned in the past.

Great ways of doing this in your revision include:

- Testing yourself using flip cards – use the ones available in the digital resources for this book.

- Testing yourself (or getting someone else to test you) using questions you've created about the topic.

- Checking your recall of previous topics by answering the Recall and connect questions in this book.

- Blurting – writing everything you can remember about a topic on a piece of paper in one colour. Then, checking what you missed out and filling it in with another colour. You can do this over and over again until you feel confident that you remember everything.

- Answering practice questions – use the ones in this book.

- Getting a good night's sleep to help consolidate your learning.

> **The importance of sleep and creating long-term memory**
>
> When you go to sleep at night, your brain goes through an important process of taking information from your short-term memory and storing it in your long-term memory.
>
> This means that getting a good night's sleep is a very important part of revision. If you don't get enough good quality sleep, you'll actually be making your revision much, much harder.

Step 2: Developing your exam skills

We've already talked about the importance of exam skills, and how many students neglect them because they're worried about covering all the knowledge.

What actually works best is developing your exam skills at the same time as learning the knowledge.

What does this look like in your studies?

- Learning something at school and your teacher setting you questions from this book or from past papers. This tests your recall as well as developing your exam skills.

- Choosing a topic to revise, learning the content and then choosing some questions from this book to test yourself at the same time as developing your exam skills.

The reason why practising your exam skills is so important is that it helps you to get good at communicating what you know and what you think. The more often you do that, the more fluent you'll become in showing what you know in your answers.

Step 3: Getting feedback

The final step is to get feedback on your work.

If you're testing yourself, the feedback is what you got wrong or what you forgot. This means you then need to go back to those things to remind yourself or improve your understanding. Then, you can test yourself again and get more feedback. You can also congratulate yourself for the things you got right – it's important to celebrate any success, big or small.

If you're doing past paper questions or the practice questions in this book, you will need to mark your work. Marking your work is one of the most important things you can do to improve. It's possible to make significant improvements in your marks in a very short space of time when you start marking your work.

Why is marking your own work so powerful? It's because it teaches you to identify the strengths and weaknesses of your own work. When you look at the mark scheme and see how it's structured, you will understand what is needed in your answers to get the results you want.

This doesn't just apply to the knowledge you demonstrate in your answers. It also applies to the language you use and whether it's appropriately subject-specific, the structure of your answer, how you present it on the page and many other factors. Understanding, practising and improving on these things are transformative for your results.

The most important thing about revision

The most important way to make your revision successful is to make it active.

Sometimes, students say they're revising when they sit staring at their textbook or notes for hours at a time. However, this is a really ineffective way to revise because it's passive. In order to make knowledge and skills stick, you need to be doing something like the suggestions in the following diagram. That's why testing yourself and pushing yourself to answer questions that test higher-level thinking skills are so effective. At times, you might actually be able to feel the physical changes happening in your brain as you develop this new knowledge and these new skills. That doesn't come about without effort.

The important thing to remember is that while active revision feels much more like hard work than passive revision, you don't actually need to do nearly as much of it. That's because you remember knowledge and skills when you use active revision. When you use passive revision, it is much, much harder for the knowledge and skills to stick in your memory.

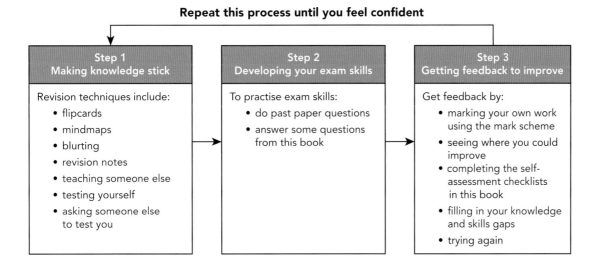

Repeat this process until you feel confident

Step 1 Making knowledge stick	Step 2 Developing your exam skills	Step 3 Getting feedback to improve
Revision techniques include: • flipcards • mindmaps • blurting • revision notes • teaching someone else • testing yourself • asking someone else to test you	To practise exam skills: • do past paper questions • answer some questions from this book	Get feedback by: • marking your own work using the mark scheme • seeing where you could improve • completing the self-assessment checklists in this book • filling in your knowledge and skills gaps • trying again

How to improve your exam skills

This book helps you to improve in eight different areas of exam skills, which are divided across three categories. These skills are highlighted in this book in the Exam skills focus at the start of each chapter and developed throughout the book using targeted questions, advice and reflections.

1 **Understand the questions: what are you being asked to do?**

   • Know your question types.

   • Understand command words.

   • Work with mark scheme awareness.

2 **How to answer questions brilliantly**

   • Understand connections between concepts.

   • Keep to time.

   • Know what a good answer looks like.

3 **Give yourself the best chance of success**

   • Reflection on progress.

   • How to manage test anxiety.

Understand the questions: what are you being asked to do?

Know your question types

In any exam, there will be a range of different question types. These different question types will test different types of thinking skills from Bloom's Taxonomy.

It is very important that you learn to recognise different question types. If you do lots of past papers, over time you will begin to recognise the structure of the paper for each of your subjects. You will know which types of questions may come first and which ones are more likely to come at the end of the paper. You can also complete past paper questions in the Exam practice sections in this book for additional practice.

You will also recognise the differences between questions worth a lower number of marks and questions worth more marks. The key differences are:

- how much you will need to write in your answer
- how sophisticated your answer needs to be in terms of the detail you give and the depth of thinking you show.

Types of questions

1   Multiple-choice questions

Multiple-choice questions are generally worth smaller numbers of marks. You will be given several possible answers to the question, and you will have to work out which one is correct using your knowledge and skills.

There is a chance of you getting the right answer with multiple-choice questions even if you don't know the answer. This is why you must **always give an answer for multiple-choice questions** as it means there is a chance you will earn the mark.

Multiple-choice questions are often harder than they appear. The possible answers can be very similar to each other. This means you must be confident in how you work out answers or have a high level of understanding to tell the difference between the possible answers.

Being confident in your subject knowledge and doing lots of practice multiple-choice questions will set you up for success. Use the resources in this book and the accompanying online resources to build your confidence.

This example of a multiple-choice question is worth one mark. You can see that all the answers have one part in common with at least one other answer. For example, palisade cells is included in three of the possible answers. That's why you have to really know the detail of your content knowledge to do well with multiple-choice questions.

Which two types of cells are found in plant leaves?

    A   Palisade mesophyll and stomata

    B   Palisade mesophyll and root hair

    C   Stomata and chloroplast

    D   Chloroplast and palisade mesophyll

2 Questions requiring longer-form answers

Questions requiring longer-form answers need you to write out your answer yourself.

With these questions, take careful note of how many marks are available and how much space you've been given for your answer. These two things will give you a good idea about how much you should say and how much time you should spend on the question.

A rough rule to follow is to write one sentence, or make one point, for each mark that is available. You will get better and better at these longer form questions the more you practise them.

In this example of a history question, you can see it is worth four marks. It is not asking for an explanation, just for you to list Lloyd George's aims. Therefore, you need to make four correct points in order to get full marks.

What were Lloyd George's aims during negotiations leading to the Treaty of Versailles? [4]

3 Essay questions

Essay questions are the longest questions you will be asked to answer in an exam. They examine the higher-order thinking skills from Bloom's Taxonomy such as analysis, synthesis and evaluation.

To do well in essay questions, you need to talk about what you know, giving your opinion, comparing one concept or example to another, and evaluating your own ideas or the ones you're discussing in your answer.

You also need to have a strong structure and logical argument that guides the reader through your thought process. This usually means having an introduction, some main body paragraphs that discuss one point at a time, and a conclusion.

Essay questions are usually level-marked. This means that you don't get one mark per point you make. Instead, you're given marks for the quality of the ideas you're sharing as well as how well you present those ideas through the subject-specific language you use and the structure of your essay.

Practising essays and becoming familiar with the mark scheme is the only way to get really good at them.

Understand command words

What are command words?

Command words are the most important words in every exam question. This is because command words tell you what you need to do in your answer. Do you remember Bloom's Taxonomy? Command words tell you which thinking skill you need to demonstrate in the answer to each question.

Two very common command words are **describe** and **explain**.

When you see the command word describe in a question, you're being asked to show lower-order thinking skills like knowledge and understanding. The question will either be worth fewer marks, or you will need to make more points if it is worth more marks.

The command word explain is asking you to show higher-order thinking skills. When you see the command word explain, you need to be able to say how or why something happens.

You need to understand all of the relevant command words for the subjects you are taking. Ask your teacher where to find them if you are not sure. It's best not to try to memorise the list of command words, but to become familiar with what command words are asking for by doing lots of practice questions and marking your own work.

How to work with command words

When you first see an exam question, read it through once. Then, read it through again and identify the command word(s). Underline the command word(s) to make it clear to yourself which they are every time you refer back to the question.

You may also want to identify the **content** words in the question and underline them with a different colour. Content words tell you which area of knowledge you need to draw on to answer the question.

In this example, command words are shown in red and content words in blue:

1   **a**   Explain **four** reasons why governments might support business start-ups.   [8]

> *Adapted from Cambridge IGCSE Business Studies (0450)*
> *Q1a Paper 21 June 2022*

Marking your own work using the mark scheme will help you get even better at understanding command words and knowing how to give good answers for each.

Work with mark scheme awareness

The most transformative thing that any student can do to improve their marks is to work with mark schemes. This means using mark schemes to mark your own work at every opportunity.

Many students are very nervous about marking their own work as they do not feel experienced or qualified enough. However, being brave enough to try to mark your own work and taking the time to get good at it will improve your marks hugely.

Why marking your own work makes such a big difference

Marking your own work can help you to improve your answers in the following ways:

1   **Answering the question**

Having a deep and detailed understanding of what is required by the question enables you to answer the question more clearly and more accurately.

It can also help you to give the required information using fewer words and in less time, as you can avoid including unrelated points or topics in your answer.

2   **Using subject-specific vocabulary**

Every subject has subject-specific vocabulary. This includes technical terms for objects or concepts in a subject, such as mitosis and meiosis in biology. It also includes how you talk about the subject, using appropriate vocabulary that may differ from everyday language. For example, in any science subject you might be asked to describe the trend on a graph.

Your answer could say it 'goes up fast' or your answer could say it 'increases rapidly'. You would not get marks for saying 'it goes up fast', but you would for saying it 'increases rapidly'. This is the difference between everyday language and formal, scientific language.

When you answer lots of practice questions, you become fluent in the language specific to your subject.

3   Knowing how much to write

It's very common for students to either write too much or too little to answer questions. Becoming familiar with the mark schemes for many different questions will help you to gain a better understanding of how much you need to write in order to get a good mark.

4   Structuring your answer

There are often clues in questions about how to structure your answer. However, mark schemes give you an even stronger idea of the structure you should use in your answers.

For example, if a question says:

'Describe and explain two reasons why…'

You can give a clear answer by:

- Describing reason 1

- Explaining reason 1

- Describing reason 2

- Explaining reason 2

Having a very clear structure will also make it easier to identify where you have earned marks. This means that you're more likely to be awarded the number of marks you deserve.

5   Keeping to time

Answering the question, using subject-specific vocabulary, knowing how much to write and giving a clear structure to your answer will all help you to keep to time in an exam. You will not waste time by writing too much for any answer. Therefore, you will have sufficient time to give a good answer to every question.

How to answer exam questions brilliantly

Understand connections between concepts

One of the higher-level thinking skills in Bloom's Taxonomy is **synthesis**. Synthesis means making connections between different areas of knowledge. You may have heard about synoptic links. Making synoptic links is the same as showing the thinking skill of synthesis.

Exam questions that ask you to show your synthesis skills are usually worth the highest number of marks on an exam paper. To write good answers to these questions, you need to spend time thinking about the links between the topics you've studied **before** you arrive in your exam. A great way of doing this is using mind maps.

How to create a mind map

To create a mind map:

1 Use a large piece of paper and several different coloured pens.

2 Write the name of your subject in the middle. Then, write the key topic areas evenly spaced around the edge, each with a different colour.

3 Then, around each topic area, start to write the detail of what you can remember. If you find something that is connected with something you studied in another topic, you can draw a line linking the two things together.

This is a good way of practising your retrieval of information as well as linking topics together.

Answering synoptic exam questions

You will recognise questions that require you to make links between concepts because they have a higher number of marks. You will have practised them using this book and the accompanying resources.

To answer a synoptic exam question:

1 **Identify the command and content words.** You are more likely to find command words like **discuss** and **explain** in these questions. They might also have phrases like 'the connection between'.

2 **Make a plan for your answer.** It is worth taking a short amount of time to think about what you're going to write in your answer. Think carefully about what information you're going to put in, the links between the different pieces of information and how you're going to structure your answer to make your ideas clear.

3 **Use linking words and phrases in your answer.** For example, 'therefore', 'because', 'due to', 'since' or 'this means that'.

Here is an example of an English Literature exam question that requires you to make synoptic links in your answer.

1 Discuss Carol Ann Duffy's exploration of childhood in her poetry. Refer to two poems in your answer. [25]

Content words are shown in blue; command words are shown in red.

This question is asking you to explore the theme of childhood in Duffy's poetry. You need to choose two of her poems to refer to in your answer. This means you need a good knowledge of her poetry, and to be familiar with her exploration of childhood, so that you can easily select two poems that will give you plenty to say in your answer.

Keep to time

Managing your time in exams is really important. Some students do not achieve to the best of their abilities because they run out of time to answer all the questions. However, if you manage your time well, you will be able to attempt every question on the exam paper.

Why is it important to attempt all the questions on an exam paper?

If you attempt every question on a paper, you have the best chance of achieving the highest mark you are capable of.

Students who manage their time poorly in exams will often spend far too long on some questions and not even attempt others. Most students are unlikely to get full marks on many questions, but you will get zero marks for the questions you don't answer. You can maximise your marks by giving an answer to every question.

Minutes per mark

The most important way to keep to time is knowing how many minutes you can spend on each mark.

For example, if your exam paper has 90 marks available and you have 90 minutes, you know there is 1 mark per minute.

Therefore, if you have a 5 mark question, you should spend five minutes on it.

Sometimes, you can give a good answer in less time than you have budgeted using the minutes per mark technique. If this happens, you will have more time to spend on questions that use higher-order thinking skills, or more time on checking your work.

How to get faster at answering exam questions

The best way to get faster at answering exam questions is to do lots of practice. You should practise each question type that will be in your exam, marking your own work, so that you know precisely how that question works and what is required by the question. Use the questions in this book to get better and better at answering each question type.

Use the 'Slow, Slow, Quick' technique to get faster.

Take your time answering questions when you first start practising them. You may answer them with the support of the textbook, your notes or the mark scheme. These things will support you with your content knowledge, the language you use in your answer and the structure of your answer.

Every time you practise this question type, you will get more confident and faster. You will become experienced with this question type, so that it is easy for you to recall the subject knowledge and write it down using the correct language and a good structure.

Calculating marks per minute

Use this calculation to work out how long you have for each mark:

Total time in the exam / Number of marks available = Minutes per mark

Calculate how long you have for a question worth more than one mark like this:

Minutes per mark × Marks available for this question = Number of minutes for this question

What about time to check your work?

It is a very good idea to check your work at the end of an exam. You need to work out if this is feasible with the minutes per mark available to you. If you're always rushing to finish the questions, you shouldn't budget checking time. However, if you usually have time to spare, then you can budget checking time.

To include checking time in your minutes per mark calculation:

(Total time in the exam – Checking time) / Number of marks available = Minutes per mark

Know what a good answer looks like

It is much easier to give a good answer if you know what a good answer looks like.

Use these methods to know what a good answer looks like.

1 **Sample answers** – you can find sample answers in these places:

    - from your teacher

    - written by your friends or other members of your class

    - in this book.

2 **Look at mark schemes** – mark schemes are full of information about what you should include in your answers. Get familiar with mark schemes to gain a better understanding of the type of things a good answer would contain.

3 **Feedback from your teacher** – if you are finding it difficult to improve your exam skills for a particular type of question, ask your teacher for detailed feedback. You should also look at their comments on your work in detail.

Give yourself the best chance of success

Reflection on progress

As you prepare for your exam, it's important to reflect on your progress. Taking time to think about what you're doing well and what could be improved brings more focus to your revision. Reflecting on progress also helps you to continuously improve your knowledge and exam skills.

How do you reflect on progress?

Use the 'reflection' feature in this book to help you reflect on your progress during your exam preparation. Then, at the end of each revision session, take a few minutes to think about the following:

	What went well? What would you do the same next time?	What didn't go well? What would you do differently next time?
Your subject knowledge		
How you revised your subject knowledge – did you use active retrieval techniques?		
Your use of subject-specific and academic language		
Understanding the question by identifying command words and content words		
Giving a clear structure to your answer		
Keeping to time		
Marking your own work		

Remember to check for silly mistakes – things like missing the units out after you carefully calculated your answer.

Use the mark scheme to mark your own work. Every time you mark your own work, you will be recognising the good and bad aspects of your work, so that you can progressively give better answers over time.

When do you need to come back to this topic or skill?

Earlier in this section of the book, we talked about revision skills and the importance of spaced retrieval. When you reflect on your progress, you need to think about how soon you need to return to the topic or skill you've just been focusing on.

For example, if you were really disappointed with your subject knowledge, it would be a good idea to do some more active retrieval and practice questions on this topic tomorrow. However, if you did really well you can feel confident you know this topic and come back to it again in three weeks' or a month's time.

The same goes for exam skills. If you were disappointed with how you answered the question, you should look at some sample answers and try this type of question again soon. However, if you did well, you can move on to other types of exam questions.

Improving your memory of subject knowledge

Sometimes students slip back into using passive revision techniques, such as only reading the coursebook or their notes, rather than also using active revision techniques, like testing themselves using flip cards or blurting.

You can avoid this mistake by observing how well your learning is working as you revise. You should be thinking to yourself, 'Am I remembering this? Am I understanding this? Is this revision working?'

If the answer to any of those questions is 'no', then you need to change what you're doing to revise this particular topic. For example, if you don't understand, you could look up your topic in a different textbook in the school library to see if a different explanation helps. Or you could see if you can find a video online that brings the idea to life.

You are in control

When you're studying for exams it's easy to think that your teachers are in charge. However, you have to remember that you are studying for your exams and the results you get will be yours and no one else's.

That means you have to take responsibility for all your exam preparation. You have the power to change how you're preparing if what you're doing isn't working. You also have control over what you revise and when: you can make sure you focus on your weaker topics and skills to improve your achievement in the subject.

This isn't always easy to do. Sometimes you have to find an inner ability that you have not used before. But, if you are determined enough to do well, you can find what it takes to focus, improve and keep going.

What is test anxiety?

Do you get worried or anxious about exams? Does your worry or anxiety impact how well you do in tests and exams?

Test anxiety is part of your natural stress response.

The stress response evolved in animals and humans many thousands of years ago to help keep them alive. Let's look at an example.

The stress response in the wild

Imagine an impala grazing in the grasslands of east Africa. It's happily and calmly eating grass in its herd in what we would call the parasympathetic state of rest and repair.

Then the impala sees a lion. The impala suddenly panics because its life is in danger. This state of panic is also known as the stressed or sympathetic state. The sympathetic state presents itself in three forms: flight, fight and freeze.

The impala starts to run away from the lion. Running away is known as the flight stress response.

The impala might not be fast enough to run away from the lion. The lion catches it but has a loose grip. The impala struggles to try to get away. This struggle is the fight stress response.

However, the lion gets an even stronger grip on the impala. Now the only chance of the impala surviving is playing dead. The impala goes limp, its heart rate and breathing slows. This is called the freeze stress response. The lion believes that it has killed the impala so it drops the impala to the ground. Now the impala can switch back into the flight response and run away.

The impala is now safe – the different stages of the stress response have saved its life.

What has the impala got to do with your exams?

When you feel test anxiety, you have the same physiological stress responses as an impala being hunted by a lion. Unfortunately, the human nervous system cannot tell the difference between a life-threatening situation, such as being chased by a lion, and the stress of taking an exam.

If you understand how the stress response works in the human nervous system, you will be able to learn techniques to reduce test anxiety.

The role of the vagus nerve in test anxiety

The vagus nerve is the part of your nervous system that determines your stress response. Vagus means 'wandering' in Latin, so the vagus nerve is also known as the 'wandering nerve'. The vagus nerve wanders from your brain, down each side of your body, to nearly all your organs, including your lungs, heart, kidneys, liver, digestive system and bladder.

If you are in a stressful situation, like an exam, your vagus nerve sends a message to all these different organs to activate their stress response. Here are some common examples:

- **Heart** beats faster.
- **Kidneys** produce more adrenaline so that you can run, making you fidgety and distracted.
- **Digestive system** and **bladder** want to eliminate all waste products so that energy can be used for fight or flight.

If you want to feel calmer about your revision and exams, you need to do two things to help you move into the parasympathetic, or rest and repair, state:

1 Work with your vagus nerve to send messages of safety through your body.

2 Change your perception of the test so that you see it as safe and not dangerous.

How to cope with test anxiety

1 Be well prepared

Good preparation is the most important part of managing test anxiety. The better your preparation, the more confident you will be. If you are confident, you will not perceive the test or exam as dangerous, so the sympathetic nervous system responses of fight, flight and freeze are less likely to happen.

This book is all about helping you to be well prepared and building your confidence in your knowledge and ability to answer exam questions well. Working through the knowledge recall questions will help you to become more confident in your knowledge of the subject. The practice questions and exam skills questions will help you to become more confident in communicating your knowledge in an exam.

To be well prepared, look at the advice in the rest of this chapter and use it as you work through the questions in this book.

2 Work with your vagus nerve

The easiest way to work with your vagus nerve to tell it that you're in a safe situation is through your breathing. This means breathing deeply into the bottom of your lungs, so that your stomach expands, and then breathing out for longer than you breathed in. You can do this with counting.

Breathe in deeply, expanding your abdomen, for the count of four; breathe out drawing your navel back towards your spine for the count of five, six or seven. Repeat this at least three times. However, you can do it for as long as it takes for you to feel calm.

The important thing is that you breathe out for longer than you breathe in. This is because when you breathe in, your heart rate increases slightly, and when you breathe out, your heart rate decreases slightly. If you're spending more time breathing out overall, you will be decreasing your heart rate over time.

3 Feel it

Anxiety is an uncomfortable, difficult thing to feel. That means that many people try to run away from anxious feelings. However, this means the stress just gets stored in your body for you to feel later.

When you feel anxious, follow these four steps:

1 Pause.

2 Place one hand on your heart and one hand on your stomach.

3 Notice what you're feeling.

4 Stay with your feelings.

What you will find is that if you are willing to experience what you feel for a minute or two, the feeling of anxiety will usually pass very quickly.

4 Write or talk it out

If your thoughts are moving very quickly, it is often better to get them out of your mind and on to paper.

You could take a few minutes to write down everything that comes through your mind, then rip up your paper and throw it away. If you don't like writing, you can speak aloud alone or to someone you trust.

Other ways to break the stress cycle

Exercise and movement	Being friendly	Laughter
• Run or walk. • Dance. • Lift weights. • Yoga. Anything that involves moving your body is helpful.	• Chat to someone in your study break. • Talk to the cashier when you buy your lunch.	• Watch or listen to a funny show on TV or online. • Talk with someone who makes you laugh. • Look at photos of fun times.
Have a hug	Releasing emotions	Creativity
• Hug a friend or relative. • Cuddle a pet e.g. a cat. Hug for 20 seconds or until you feel calm and relaxed.	It is healthy to release negative or sad emotions. Crying is often a quick way to get rid of these difficult feelings so if you feel like you need to cry, allow it.	• Paint, draw or sketch. • Sew, knit or crochet. • Cook, build something.

If you have long-term symptoms of anxiety, it is important to tell someone you trust and ask for help.

Your perfect revision session

1 Intention

What do you want to achieve in this revision session?

- Choose an area of knowledge or an exam skill that you want to focus on.
- Choose some questions from this book that focus on this knowledge area or skill.
- Gather any other resources you will need e.g. pen, paper, flashcards, coursebook.

2 Focus

Set your focus for the session

- Remove distractions from your study area e.g. leave your phone in another room.
- Write down on a piece of paper or sticky note the knowledge area or skill you're intending to focus on.
- Close your eyes and take three deep breaths, with the exhale longer than the inhale.

3 Revision

Revise your knowledge and understanding

- To improve your knowledge and understanding of the topic, use your coursebook, notes or flashcards, including active learning techniques.
- To improve your exam skills, look at previous answers, teacher feedback, mark schemes, sample answers or examiners' reports.

4 Practice

Answer practice questions

- Use the questions in this book, or in the additional online resources, to practise your exam skills.
- If the exam is soon, do this in timed conditions without the support of the coursebook or your notes.
- If the exam is a long time away, you can use your notes and resources to help you.

5 Feedback

Mark your answers

- Use mark schemes to mark your work.
- Reflect on what you've done well and what you could do to improve next time.

6 Next steps

What have you learned about your progress from this revision session? What do you need to do next?

- What did you do well? Feel good about these things, and know it's safe to set these things aside for a while.
- What do you need to work on? How are you going to improve? Make a plan to get better at the things you didn't do well or didn't know.

7 Rest

Take a break

- Do something completely different to rest: get up, move or do something creative or practical.
- Remember that rest is an important part of studying, as it gives your brain a chance to integrate your learning.

1 States of matter

In order to be confident when approaching an exam, it's necessary to be aware of exam skills required and to practise them regularly. Each chapter will help you to focus on the skills and knowledge you need to demonstrate and to give you practice in using them.

When you read an exam question, look carefully at the command word used. It's important to understand what each command word means and what it is asking you to do.

In this chapter, look for questions with the command word 'explain'. Check your answers against those provided to make sure you fully understand this command word.

| Explain | set out purposes or reasons/make the relationships between things evident/provide reasons why and/or how and support with relevant evidence. |

1.1 States of matter

Copy and complete the following sentences.

1 **a** The three states of matter are ………………., ……………….., and ……………… .

    b Changing the ……………….. and ……………….. can change the state at which a substance exists.

    c Name a factor that affects the boiling point and melting point of a substance.

    d A ……………….. consists of only one type of material with no impurities present.

2 State two differences between evaporation and boiling. **[Total: 2]**

> **UNDERSTAND THESE TERMS**
> - boiling
> - condensation
> - evaporation
> - liquid
> - matter
> - melting point
> - pure substance
> - volatility

1.2 Kinetic particle theory of matter

1 What is the smallest particle of an element that can take part in a chemical reaction?

2 What is an element?
    A a substance consisting of one type of atom only
    B two or more atoms combined together physically
    C two or more atoms combined together chemically
    D an electrically-charged particle

3 Copy and complete the following sentence. An ……………….. reaction gives out heat, while an ……………….. reaction absorbs heat.

4 Explain the kinetic particle theory. **[Total: 3]**

> **UNDERSTAND THESE TERMS**
> - atom
> - molecule
> - intermolecular forces

1.3 Mixtures of substances and diffusion

1 How is a mixture formed?

Copy and complete the following sentences.

2 a A substance that can dissolve in a solvent is said to be ...., while a substance that cannot dissolve in a solvent is known as ....

   b A solute dissolving in a solvent will produce a ....

   c .... is the process by which different liquids mix as a result of the random motion of the particles.

3 Explain why the temperature remains constant during the processes of boiling and melting.

[Total: 2]

UNDERSTAND THESE TERMS
• diffusion
• insoluble
• mixture
• precipitation
• soluble
• solute
• solution
• solvent
• suspension

REFLECTION

At the end of this chapter, how confident do you feel answering 'explain' questions? Do you think you could explain the three states of matter using the kinetic particle theory to a friend?

What strategies could help you to visualise particles like atoms, molecules and ions?

SELF-ASSESSMENT CHECKLIST

Let's revisit the Knowledge focus and Exam skills focus for this chapter.

Decide how confident you are with each statement.

Now I can:	Show it	Needs more work	Almost there	Confident to move on
describe that matter can exist in three different states: solid, liquid or gas	Draw particle diagrams to depict solids, liquids and gases, and use them to explain the differences between the three states of matter.			
understand that substances can change state depending on the physical conditions	Draw heating and cooling curves and use them to explain the changes that occur during the two processes.			

CONTINUED

Now I can:	Show it	Needs more work	Almost there	Confident to move on
understand that matter is made up of very small particles such as atoms or molecules	Write a paragraph describing how matter is made up of these types of particles: atoms, molecules or ions.			
see how changes in temperature produce changes of state by affecting the motion of the particles involved	Write a paragraph to describe how temperature increases the motion of the particles.			
describe the structure of the physical states in terms of the arrangement and movement of particles	Write a paragraph to explain the differences between the three states of matter using kinetic particle theory.			
describe how changes in temperature and pressure affect the volume of a gas	Use the kinetic particle theory to explain the effects of changing temperature and pressure on the volumes of gases.			
explain diffusion in terms of the movement of particles	Explain that diffusion does not take place in solids and describe diffusion when bromine gas is placed in a glass jar with a lid.			
think about how the movement of particles (kinetic particle theory) helps explain how changes of state happen	Write a paragraph to explain intermolecular forces and shape in terms of kinetic particle theory.			
understand the effects of changes in temperature and pressure on the volume of a gas	State the effects of changing temperature and pressure on the volume of a gas.			
describe how the molecular mass of particles in a gas affects the rate of diffusion	Describe the effect of relative molecular mass on the rate of diffusion of a gas.			

CONTINUED

Now I can:	Show it	Needs more work	Almost there	Confident to move on
show that I understand the command word 'explain' and answer an 'explain' question.	Compare your written answers to the 'explain' questions in this chapter to the answers provided to make sure that you understood the command word correctly.			

2 Atomic structure

In this chapter you will practise answering questions with the command words 'describe' and 'determine' and how answers to these types of questions should be presented. It is important that you understand what a command word is instructing you to do.

Describe	state the points of a topic/give characteristics and main features.
Determine	establish an answer using the information available.

In addition to understanding command words, recognising different question types is as important. These may include multiple choice questions (MCQs), short answer questions, extended response questions and others. In this chapter, you will practise by distinguishing between some of these questions types and understand what you are required to do for each:

- Short answer questions: carry fewer marks and may contain an indication in the question as to how many points should be made, e.g. 'State one difference…'.

- Long answer questions: carry more marks and require a structured answer, e.g. 'Give reasons…'.

2.1 Atoms and elements

1   Silicon is an element. Write a sentence to describe silicon that includes each word in the box.

atoms	particles	element

2

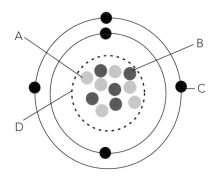

Figure 2.1

a   Figure 2.1 shows the structure of an atom. Identify the missing labels, **A** to **D**.   [4]

b   Identify the element shown in Figure 2.1.   [1]

[Total: 5]

3   Atoms are made of the subatomic particles electrons, protons and neutrons.

Describe **one** similarity and **one** difference between these subatomic particles in terms of their relative mass, relative charge or location in the atom.   **[Total: 2]**

≪ RECALL AND CONNECT 1 ≪

What is the difference between an atom and a molecule?

2.2 Isotopes

1 Here is some information for an atom.

$$^{7}_{3}\text{Li}$$

Copy and complete the following sentences using words or numbers from the box.

4 proton number 3 lithium mass number Li 3

The element shown is ....
This is represented by the chemical symbol, ...
The .... determines which element it is in the Periodic Table.

The number 7 represents the ....
The numbers 7 and 3 tell us that there are .... protons, ...
electrons and .... neutrons.

2 Copy and complete Figure 2.2 to compare the mass numbers and numbers of subatomic particles in the isotopes of carbon, $^{12}_{6}\text{C}$ and $^{14}_{6}\text{C}$.

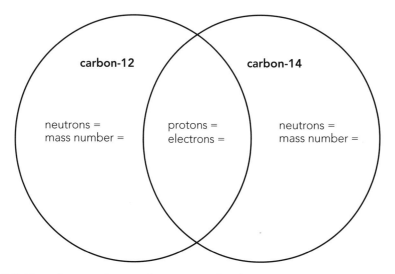

Figure 2.2: Venn diagram showing the isotopes of carbon

3 $^{24}_{12}$Mg and $^{26}_{12}$Mg are isotopes of magnesium.

  a Define the term *isotopes*.   [1]

  b $^{24}_{12}$Mg reacts with dilute hydrochloric acid to form magnesium chloride and hydrogen gas.

   i Predict the outcome when $^{24}_{12}$Mg is replaced with its isotope, $^{26}_{12}$Mg.   [1]

   ii Justify your answer for part **c** i.   [1]

                                                                          [Total: 3]

2.3 Electronic configuration of elements

1 Figure 2.3 represents the electron structure of a beryllium atom, Be.

  a Write down the electronic configuration of a beryllium atom in numbers. (e.g. 2,8,4 for silicon)

  b Draw an electron structure diagram to represent a lithium atom, which has one fewer electron than beryllium.

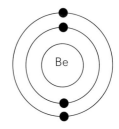

Figure 2.3: Electron structure of beryllium atom

2 The chemical properties of an element are determined by the number of outer electrons in the atom. Fluorine is found in Group 7, Period 2 of the Periodic Table.

Use the information provided to determine the number of outer electrons and number of occupied electron shells in a fluorine atom.

3 The element potassium has 19 protons. Use this information to determine the group number and period number of potassium. Give reasons for your answers.   **[Total: 4]**

REFLECTION

How confident did you feel answering the questions in this chapter? Are there any areas that you felt unsure about? Write them down.

Now write down what you will do to strengthen your learning for these areas. For example, define the term isotope and see if you are able to identify isotopes by trying out some practice questions.

How will you check that you have improved your understanding? For example, could you write down the electronic configuration of a given element using the Periodic Table? Speak to your teacher if you are confused about how to write down the electronic configuration and how to use numbers in the Periodic Table.

SELF-ASSESSMENT CHECKLIST

Let's revisit the Knowledge focus and Exam skills focus for this chapter.

Decide how confident you are with each statement.

Now I can:	Show it	Needs more work	Almost there	Confident to move on
describe how atoms are the particles that make up the different elements	Write down the relationship between atoms, particles and elements.			
study the nuclear model of the atom	Draw the nuclear model of an atom.			
describe the relative charge and mass of the proton, neutron and electron	Create a table to distinguish protons, electrons and neutrons in terms of their relative charge and mass.			
determine how the structure of any atom is defined by its proton number and mass number	Draw the electronic structure of an element based on its proton number and mass number.			
describe how the isotopes of an element have the same proton number but different numbers of neutrons	Define the term isotope.			
describe how the electrons in an atom are organised in shells around the nucleus	Draw the electronic structure of an element using its atomic number.			
see how the electronic configuration of the atoms of an element relates to its position in the Periodic Table	Write down the electronic configuration of elements in Group 1 and recognise the pattern.			
describe how the isotopes of an element all have the same chemical properties	Write down reasons for same chemical properties and different physical properties in isotopes.			
calculate the relative atomic mass of an element	Try a flip card or past paper questions to practise questions on relative atomic mass.			

CONTINUED

Now I can:	Show it	Needs more work	Almost there	Confident to move on
understand the 'describe' and 'determine' command words and answer 'describe' and 'determine' questions.	Find and answer a 'describe' question and a 'determine' question in a past paper. Check the command word definitions before answering, then check your answer against the mark scheme.			

3 Chemical bonding

In this chapter you will answer questions on:

- non-metallic substances and covalent bonding
- ions and ionic bonding
- giant structures.

EXAM SKILLS FOCUS

In this chapter you will:

- show that you understand the 'sketch' command word and can answer a 'sketch' question.

In this chapter you will practise answering questions with the command word 'sketch'.

| Sketch | make a simple freehand drawing showing the key features, taking care over proportions. |

The 'sketch' command word is often used for topics where information is shown graphically, or where simple diagrams can clearly show important ideas. For example, you may be asked to sketch different types of dot-and-cross diagrams or energy level diagrams. Sketches should be simple and show only the main features asked for in the question.

3.1 Non-metallic substances and covalent bonding

1 Copy and complete Table 3.1 using the text in the box.

mixture	element	compound

cannot be divided into simpler substances by chemical methods

consists of two or more types of elements and/or compounds

can be separated by physical methods

consists of two or more types of atoms chemically combined

can only be broken down by chemical methods

consists of only one type of atom

Table 3.1

2 Copy the table and tick (✓) the statements that correctly describe covalent bonding.

formed from sharing of one or more pairs of electrons between two atoms	
formed from strong electrostatic force of attraction between oppositely charged ions	
formed between a metal and a non-metal	
formed between non-metals	
formed when each atom contributes one electron to each bond	
found in diatomic molecules	
formed from the transfer of electrons from one atom to another	

3 Ethene, C_2H_4, is a hydrocarbon.

a Sketch a dot-and-cross diagram to show the electron arrangement in ethene, C_2H_4. Show the outer electrons only. [2]

b Explain why ethene does not conduct electricity. [1]

[Total: 3]

UNDERSTAND THESE TERMS

- element
- metals
- non-metals
- compound
- chemical formula
- chemical bonding
- diatomic molecules
- covalent bonding
- dot-and-cross diagram

3.2 Ions and ionic bonding

1   Copy and complete Figure 3.1 to show how a sodium atom and a chlorine atom combine to form the compound sodium chloride. Show the outer shell electrons only.

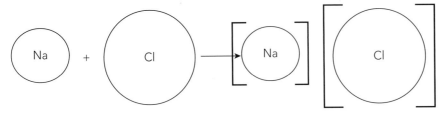

Figure 3.1: Incomplete dot-and-cross diagram

2   Magnesium oxide, MgO has a lattice structure.

   a   State the type of bonding in magnesium oxide.   [1]

   b   Sketch a dot-and-cross diagram to show the bonding in magnesium oxide.   [2]

[Total: 3]

3   Methane is a covalent compound. Sodium chloride is an ionic compound.

   a   Describe methane and sodium chloride in terms of their melting and boiling points. Justify your answer.   [3]

   b   Sodium chloride is a crystalline solid at room temperature. Explain this property in terms of its structure and bonding.   [2]

[Total: 5]

UNDERSTAND THESE TERMS
• ionic bonding
• ions
• electrostatic forces
• cation
• anion

≪ RECALL AND CONNECT 1 ≪

Ionic bonding is the electrostatic force of attraction between oppositely charged ions. What is the relative charge of a proton?

3.3 Giant structures

1   The information given in the three rows is mixed up. Match each structure to its properties and and then to its uses. Graphite has been started for you.

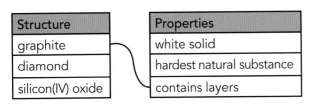

Structure	Properties	Uses
graphite	white solid	cutting tools
diamond	hardest natural substance	glass for windows
silicon(IV) oxide	contains layers	lubricants

2   Figure 3.2 shows the structure of diamond and silicon(IV) oxide.

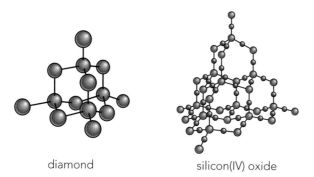

diamond   silicon(IV) oxide

Figure 3.2

a   State the type of bonding found in both structures in Figure 3.2.   [1]
b   Describe diamond and silicon(IV) oxide in terms of their structures.   [3]

[Total: 4]

3   Iron and copper are metals.

a   Sketch a labelled diagram to show the bonding in a metallic element
    such as iron or copper.   [2]
b   Metals are malleable. Explain this property in terms of structure.   [2]

[Total: 4]

« RECALL AND CONNECT 2 «

How many electrons can occupy the first shell of an atom?

UNDERSTAND THESE TERMS

- giant ionic lattice (structure)
- giant structures
- giant covalent structures
- giant metallic lattice
- 'sea' of delocalised electrons
- metallic bonding
- malleable
- ductile

REFLECTION

How did you find the 'sketch' questions in this chapter? Did you keep your sketches simple and only show the key features? Did you manage to score all 3 marks in the compare question? If not, how will you check that you have improved your understanding?

SELF-ASSESSMENT CHECKLIST

Let's revisit the Knowledge focus and Exam skills focus for this chapter.

Decide how confident you are with each statement.

Now I can:	Show it	Needs more work	Almost there	Confident to move on
outline the differences between elements, compounds and mixtures	Create a table that shows the contrast of elements, compounds and mixtures.			
understand that a covalent bond is formed by sharing a pair of outer electrons between two atoms and describe bonding in simple molecules	Sketch a dot-and-cross diagram to show the arrangement of electrons in a hydrogen molecule.			
understand the formation of ions and that an ionic bond is the strong electrostatic force of attraction between oppositely charged ions	Describe how an ionic bond is formed.			
relate the properties of simple molecular and ionic compounds to their structure and bonding	Create a table that shows the physical properties of ionic compounds and reasons for their physical properties.			
outline the giant covalent structures of diamond and graphite and relate these to their uses	Create a table that shows the physical properties and uses of diamond and graphite.			
describe bonding in more complex molecules	Sketch a dot-and-cross diagram of complex covalent molecules such as ethene and methanol.			
describe the formation of ionic bonds between metals and non-metals	Sketch a dot-and-cross diagram of sodium chloride			
explain the properties of simple molecular and ionic compounds in terms of their structure and bonding	Create a table that shows the properties of simple molecular compounds and ionic compounds in terms of their structure and bonding.			

CONTINUED

Now I can:	Show it	Needs more work	Almost there	Confident to move on
describe the giant covalent structure of silicon(IV) oxide	Write down the characteristics of the silicon(IV) oxide structure.			
describe how metallic bonding is the electrostatic attraction between the positive ions in the metallic lattice and a 'sea' of delocalised electrons between them	Sketch a labelled diagram of metallic bonding in metals that includes the positive ions and 'sea' of delocalised electrons.			
explain physical properties of metals in terms of metallic bonding	List the physical properties of metals in terms of metallic bonding.			
understand the 'sketch' command word and answer a 'sketch' question.	Compare your answers to the 'sketch' questions in this chapter with the mark schemes to see if you understand the command word correctly.			

Exam practice 1

This section contains past paper questions from previous Cambridge exams, which draw together your knowledge on a range of topics that you have covered up to this point. These questions give you the opportunity to test your knowledge and understanding. Additional past paper practice questions can be found in the accompanying digital material.

The following three questions have an example student response and commentary provided. Once you have worked through the question, read the student response and commentary. Are your answers different to the sample answers?

1 **a** For each of the following, give the name of an element from Period 3 (sodium to argon), which matches the description.

      i an element which is gaseous at room temperature and pressure   **[1]**

      ii an element used as an inert atmosphere in lamps.   **[1]**

                                                                  [Total: 2]

Cambridge IGCSE Chemistry (0620) Paper 32, Q1a, d March 2015

  b The diagram shows a blast furnace for extracting iron.

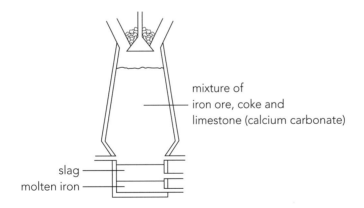

mixture of iron ore, coke and limestone (calcium carbonate)

slag

molten iron

      i How do you know from the information in the diagram that slag is less dense than molten iron?   **[Total: 1]**

Cambridge IGCSE Chemistry (0620) Paper 32, Q2a ii March 2017 c   Octane is an alkane. The table shows some properties of different alkanes.

alkane	formula	melting point/°C	boiling point/°C
methane	CH_4	−182	−164
ethane	C_2H_6	−183	−88
propane	C_3H_8	−190	−42
butane	C_4H_{10}	−138	0
pentane	C_5H_{12}	−130	36

   i   How does the boiling point of the alkanes change with the number
       of carbon atoms?   [1]
   ii Which alkane in the table is liquid at room temperature (20 °C)?
       Explain your answer.   [2]

                                                              [Total: 3]

Cambridge IGCSE Chemistry (0620) Paper 32, Q3c i, ii March 2017

Example student response	Commentary
1 a i argon	The student has identified the correct element. Chlorine is also an acceptable answer. **This answer is awarded 1 out of 1 mark.**
ii argon	The student has identified the correct element. **This answer is awarded 1 out of 1 mark.**
b i because there is more slag	The student has not correctly recognised that the amount or thickness of slag layer is irrelevant to its density. The answer should refer to the slag forming a layer above the molten iron. **This answer is awarded 0 out of 1 mark.**
c i it decreases	The student has not linked the number of carbon atoms in the molecule to the boiling point and may have misunderstood the values of the temperatures, given the negative signs. **This answer is awarded 0 out of 1 mark.**
ii butane, because it changes at 0 °C like water	The student has not correctly identified pentane. The substance must melt below 20 °C and boil above 20 °C to be liquid at this temperature. **This answer is awarded 0 out of 2 marks.**

Now you have read the commentary to the previous question, here is a similar question that you should attempt. Use the information from the previous response and commentary to guide you as you answer.

2 Chromatography can be used to separate the coloured pigments extracted from lavender flowers. The apparatus used is shown.

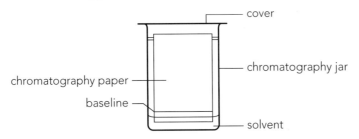

After a few minutes the solvent vapour fills the whole chromatography jar.

Use the kinetic particle model to explain this. **[Total: 3]**

Cambridge IGCSE Chemistry (0620) Paper 32, Q5e March 2017

The following question has an example student response and commentary provided. Once you have worked through the question, compare your answer to the student response and commentary.

3 The table shows some properties of the Group 1 elements.

element	melting point/°C	density in g/cm³	observations during reaction with water
lithium	181		slow bubbling no flame
sodium	98		rapid bubbling no flame
potassium	63	0.86	rapid bubbling lilac flame
rubidium		1.53	
caesium	29	1.83	explodes

a i Complete the table by predicting:

  • the melting point of rubidium

  • the density of lithium. [2]

  ii Predict the observations when rubidium reacts with water. [1]

b Deduce the electronic structure of potassium.

  Use the Periodic Table to help you. [1]

c Lithium reacts with water to produce aqueous lithium hydroxide and a gas which 'pops' with a lighted splint.

  i Name the gas which 'pops' with a lighted splint. [1]

  ii Choose **one** pH value from the list that best describes the pH of aqueous lithium hydroxide.

    Draw a circle around the correct answer.

    pH 2   pH 5   pH 7   pH 13 [1]

    iii   Lithium reacts with nitrogen.

        Complete the chemical equation for this reaction.

$$\ldots\ldots Li + N_2 \rightarrow \ldots\ldots Li_3N \qquad\qquad [2]$$

[Total: 8]

Cambridge IGCSE Chemistry (0620) Paper 31, Q4 November 2021

Example student response	Commentary
3 a i melting point 35 °C density 0.70 g/cm³	The student demonstrated a good skill of analysing the data in the table and recognising patterns in order to predict a melting point and density. *This answer is awarded 2 out of 2 marks.*
ii very rapid bubbling with flame and slight explosion	The student demonstrated a good skill of analysing the data in the table and recognising patterns in order to predict the observation. The response also shows the student's knowledge recall on the reactivity of the metals as you go down Group 1. *This answer is awarded 1 out of 1 mark.*
b 39–19 20	This question carries a total of 1 mark. To gain 1 mark, students should just indicate the answer, without any working required, to 'deduce' the electronic structure. *This answer is awarded 0 out of 1 mark.*
c i oxygen	The response showed that the student could not recall the type of test and results for the different gases, as they have stated the incorrect gas. *This answer is awarded 0 out of 1 mark.*
ii pH 13	The response showed that the student could recall the acid and base content and is also able to determine whether lithium hydroxide is an acid or a base. *This answer is awarded 1 out of 1 mark.*
iii $3Li + N_2 \rightarrow 2Li_3N$	This is a common mistake students make when balancing symbol equations. The response here showed that the student knows that there should be the same number of atoms for both the reactants and products. Hence, the student writes 3 Li when they see a subscript '3' on the right side of the Li product and writes 2 Li_3N when they see a subscript '2' on the right side of the N reactant. However, students tend to miss out the coefficient '2' which was placed on the left side of Li_3N. This coefficient '2' has to be multiplied with the number of atoms of Li and also N. *This answer is awarded 1 out of 2 marks for the correct '2' for Li_3N.*

4   Now that you have read the sample response and commentary to the previous question, rewrite your answer to any question part where you did not score highly.

The following question has an example student response and commentary provided. Once you have worked through the question, read the student response and commentary. Are your answers different to the sample answers? How are they different?

5   The table shows the masses of some ions in a 1000 cm³ sample of toothpaste.

name of ion	formula of ion	mass of ion in 1000 cm³ of toothpaste/g
ammonium	NH_4^+	0.5
calcium	Ca^{2+}	3.6
carbonate	CO_3^{2-}	2.5
chloride	Cl^-	0.9
fluoride	F^-	1.2
	Mg^{2+}	0.2
phosphate	PO_4^{3-}	28.0
sodium	Na^+	32.0
	SO_4^{2-}	10.4
tin(II)	Sn^{2+}	0.3

a   Answer these questions using only the information in the table.

   i   State which positive ion has the lowest mass in 1000 cm³ of toothpaste.   [1]

   ii   Name the compound that contains Mg^{2+} and SO_4^{2-} ions.   [1]

   iii Calculate the mass of sodium ions in 200 cm³ of toothpaste.   [1]

b   Describe a test for chloride ions.

   test:

   observations: [2]

c   Toothpaste also contains glycerol. The structure of glycerol is shown.

   Deduce the formula of glycerol to show the number of atoms of carbon, hydrogen and oxygen.   [1]

d   Glycerol is an alcohol. Ethanol is also an alcohol.

   i   Draw the structure of ethanol to show all of the atoms and all of the bonds.   [1]

   ii   Name the **two** products formed when ethanol undergoes complete combustion.   [2]

   iii Give **one** use of ethanol.   [1]

[Total: 10]

Cambridge IGCSE Chemistry (0620) Paper 32, Q2 June 2022

Example student response	Commentary
5 a i Mg^{2+}	The correct response here showed that the student was able to identify the data correctly from analysing the correct heading of the table. *This answer is awarded 1 out of 1 mark.*
ii magnesium sulfide	The response here showed that the student was able to identify Mg^{2+} correctly. However, the student was not able to recall the name of the compound ion SO_4^{2-} correctly. *This answer is awarded 0 out of 1 mark.*
iii 32g – 1000 cm^3 ? g – 200 cm^3 $32/1000 \times 200 = 6.4g$	The student showed good application of mathematical skills where they were able to use the information given in the table to identify the mass for a different volume. *This answer is awarded 1 out of 1 mark.*
b test: using sodium hydroxide observations: white precipitate	The first response on the test here shows an incorrect knowledge recall of the ions test. The answer indicated is used to test for cations instead of anions. The second response on the observation is correct. It might be a weak representation of the student's understanding as most of the ions tested with sodium hydroxide would also show a white precipitate. However, one mark is still awarded here. *This answer is awarded 1 out of 2 marks.*
c $C_3H_8O_3$	The student's response here showed a good understanding of the command term 'deduce', and also of the term 'formula', as they were able to write down the correct representation of the number of atoms. It is common for some students to write down an equation when they see the term 'formula'. *This answer is awarded 1 out of 1 mark.*
d i drawing of the structure of ethanol correctly (structure showing H—C—C—O—H with H atoms)	The response here showed a knowledge recall of the drawing of the homologous structures. The functional group is shown correctly. *This answer is awarded 1 out of 1 mark.*
ii carbon dioxide and water	The response showed a good recall of the products produced during complete combustion of an alcohol. *This answer is awarded 2 out of 2 marks.*
iii can be used as a solvent	The student demonstrated a good knowledge recall of the uses of ethanol. *This answer is awarded 1 out of 1 mark.*

6 Now that you've gone through the commentary to the previous question, try to write an improved answer to any part where you did not score highly. This will help you check if you've understood exactly why each mark has (or has not) been allocated. In your new answers, make sure you read the question and address the scope of the question.

4 Chemical formulae and equations

In this chapter you will practise your understanding of the command word 'define'. Make sure you understand what the command words 'define' and 'deduce' are instructing you to do.

| Deduce | conclude from available information. |
| Define | give precise meaning. |

'Deduce' command word questions ask you to link together ideas and information to make a conclusion. As you answer the 'deduce' question in this chapter, write down the concepts separately and then link them together to make your conclusion.

'Define' command word questions require you to give a brief definition of a term or concept. They are usually worth one mark, so should be simple recall. You should ideally answer a 'define' question by using the definition stated in the Coursebook or the syllabus for this term or process.

It is a good idea to practise writing the definitions for the key terms in the Coursebook chapters as these are the terms you could be asked to define in an exam.

4.1 Chemical names and formulae

1 Copy and complete the table with the correct elements from the list that would form positive ions (cations) or negative ions (anions).

| magnesium, Mg | sulfate, SO_4 | sulfur, S | zinc, Zn |
| oxygen, O | calcium, Ca | nitrate, NO_3 | silver, Ag |

Forming positive ions (cations)	Forming negative ions (anions)

2 Copy and complete the table with the correct compound name and formula formed from these ions.

Positive ion	Negative ion	Compound name	Compound formula
Fe^{2+}	Cl^-		
Al^{3+}	Br^-		
Na^+	N^{3-}		
K^+	CO_3^{2-}		

3 Figure 4.1 shows the structure of butanoic acid.

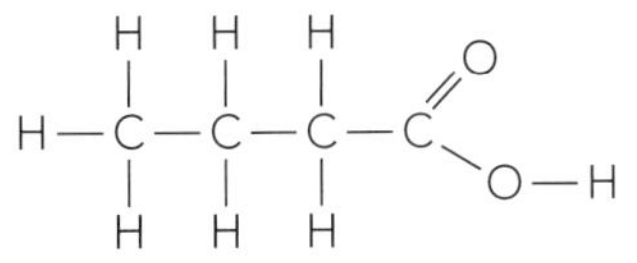

Figure 4.1

a Deduce the molecular formulae of butanoic acid from Figure 4.1. [1]

b Define the term *molecular formula of a compound*. [1]

[Total: 2]

≪ RECALL AND CONNECT 1 ≪

Charges on the ions are needed to determine the formulae of compounds. How do metal atoms form ions?

UNDERSTAND THESE TERMS

- chemical symbol
- compound ion
- empirical formula
- molecular formula

4.2 Chemical equations for reactions

1 Construct a balanced symbol equation for the reaction between each of the following pairs of reactants.

   a magnesium and oxygen

   b sodium hydroxide and hydrochloric acid

   c calcium and water

   d aluminum and zinc chloride

2 The chemical reaction between lithium metal and water is represented in a symbol equation as below.

$$\text{.......Li (....)} + \text{.......H}_2\text{O (....)} \rightarrow \text{.......LiOH (....)} + \text{H}_2\text{(....)}$$

   a Give the name of the compound formed, LiOH. [1]

   b Balance the symbol equation above by adding the correct number in front of the formulae. [1]

   c Give the missing state symbols for the reactants and products in the symbol equation above. [1]

   [Total: 3]

3 Here is a balanced symbol equation.

$$\text{K}_2\text{SO}_4 \text{ (aq)} + \text{Ca(NO}_3)_2 \text{ (aq)} \rightarrow \text{CaSO}_4 \text{ (s)} + 2\text{KNO}_3 \text{ (aq)}$$

   a Write the word equation for the balanced symbol equation. [1]

   b Write the ionic equation for the balanced symbol equation. [1]

   [Total: 2]

UNDERSTAND THESE TERMS

- balanced chemical (symbol) equation
- ionic equation
- products
- reactants
- state symbols
- word equation

4.3 Relative masses of atoms and molecules

1   Copy and complete the table by calculating the relative molecular (or formula) mass. Show your working.

Element/compound	Relative molecular (or formula) mass (M_r)/g/mol
H H	
O O	
H O H	
H N̈ H H	

2   Figure 4.2 shows the structure of a compound.

   a   Determine the chemical formulae of the compound shown in Figure 4.2.   [1]

   b   Define the term *relative molecular mass.*   [1]

   c   Calculate the relative molecular mass, M_r, of the compound in Figure 4.2.   [1]

                [Total: 3]

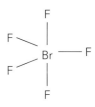

Figure 4.2

3   Sodium reacts with oxygen to form sodium oxide.
The balanced symbol equation for the reaction is:

$$4Na + O_2 \rightarrow 2Na_2O$$

   a   Calculate the relative formula mass, M_r, of Na_2O. Use the Periodic Table to help you.   [1]

   b   Calculate the mass of Na_2O formed when 8 g of oxygen is reacted with sodium.   [2]

                [Total: 3]

≪ RECALL AND CONNECT 2 ≪

Diamond is a giant covalent structure which is is made up of carbon atoms where each carbon atom is joined to four other carbon atoms by strong covalent bonds in a giant covalent structure. Name **one** use of diamond.

REFLECTION

How well did you answer the questions on chemical equations and formulae? Was it easy to recall the information you needed or was there a gap in your knowledge? If there was, then think about what techniques would help with this. You may decide to try and memorise the key terms from this chapter, or to read the chapter again and make notes or draw diagrams that would help your learning.

How confident are you that you can construct a balanced symbol equation for the reaction between sodium hydroxide and hydrochloric acid? If you find this difficult, revisit the section in this chapter and work out what would help you to strengthen your learning in this area.

SELF-ASSESSMENT CHECKLIST

Let's revisit the Knowledge focus and Exam skills focus for this chapter.

Decide how confident you are with each statement.

Now I can:	Show it	Needs more work	Almost there	Confident to move on
understand how to write the chemical formulae of elements and compounds	Write a step-by-step method describing how to determine the chemical formulae of elements and compounds (e.g. nitrogen, carbon dioxide).			
define the molecular formula as the number and type of different atoms in one molecule	Determine the number of atoms in a given molecule based on a diagram (e.g. hexane).			
deduce the formula of simple covalent compounds	Write a step-by-step method describing how to determine the chemical formulae of compounds (e.g. water, carbon dioxide).			

CONTINUED

Now I can:	Show it	Needs more work	Almost there	Confident to move on
explore how to write word and balanced symbol equations, including state symbols	Practise exam skill questions on constructing word and balanced symbol equations, including state symbols.			
describe the relative atomic mass (A_r) and understand how to use A_r to calculate the relative molecular (or formula) mass (M_r)	Write down the definition of the term relative atomic mass and calculate the relative molecular mass of given molecules (e.g. CO_2).			
deduce the formula of ionic compounds	Write a step-by-step method describing how to determine the chemical formulae of ionic compounds (e.g. magnesium bromide, sodium oxide).			
understand how the empirical formula of a compound is the simplest whole number ratio of the different atoms or ions present	Write down the definition of the term empirical formula.			
understand how to write ionic equations and deduce symbol equations for chemical reactions	Practise exam skill questions on constructing ionic equations.			
understand the 'define' and 'deduce' command words and answer 'define' and 'deduce' questions.	Practise similar questions that use the command word 'deduce' and compare your written answers to the answers provided, and use the glossary and syllabus to help you find and learn the definitions for key words and terms.			

5 Chemical calculations

In this chapter, pay attention to the 'calculate' and 'show (that)' questions and ensure you know what these command words mean.

Calculate	work out from given facts, figures or information.
Show (that)	provide structured evidence that leads to a given result.

Remember to show all the steps in your working when answering 'calculate' questions because you may receive marks for using the correct method, even if you use the wrong values. Practise showing all your working as you answer the 'calculate' questions in this chapter.

A good answer for 'calculate' questions includes:

* showing the mathematical steps you took leading to the answer

* using appropriate units

* using an appropriate number of significant figures asked for in the question.

5.1 The mole and Avogadro's constant

1 What is the number of carbon atoms present in 0.5 moles of oxalic acid $(C_2H_2O_4)$?

2 What is the number of Cu^+ ions in two moles of copper(I) oxide?

3 Show that two of the following contain the same number of molecules.

2.0 g of methane, CH_4

8.0 g of oxygen, O_2

2.0 g of ozone, O_3

8.0 g of sulfur dioxide, SO_2

[Total: 2]

> **UNDERSTAND THESE TERMS**
>
> • molar mass
> • Avogadro's constant

≪ RECALL AND CONNECT 1 ≪

An atom is a particle. Describe the structure of the atom.

5.2 The mole and chemical equations

1 Balance the following symbol equation:

$$N_2 + \text{........ } H_2 \rightleftharpoons \text{........ } NH_3$$

2 What term is used for the formula showing the simplest ratio of number of atoms of each element in a compound?

3 What is the total number of ions present in one formula unit of $Al_2(SO_4)_3$?

4 How many moles of HCl are needed to react with 0.87 moles of Al?

5   Aluminium bromide can be prepared by the reaction of aluminium metal with bromine gas, as shown by the equation:

$$2Al + 3Br_2 \rightleftharpoons 2AlBr_3$$

For each of the following questions 5.6 mol of aluminium reacts with 4.4 mol of bromine. Use the Periodic Table for relevant information.

a   Calculate the maximum mass of aluminium bromide that is produced from 5.6 moles of Al.   [2]

b   Calculate the maximum mass of aluminium bromide that is produced from 4.4 moles of bromine.   [2]

c   Use your answers to **a** and **b** to answer the following questions:

   i   The limiting reactant is …………………………… .   [1]

   ii   The excess reactant is …………………………… .   [1]

   iii   The actual amount of product produced is …………………………… .   [1]

[Total: 7]

> ### UNDERSTAND THESE TERMS
>
> - limiting reactant
> - percentage composition
> - molar gas volume

REFLECTION

Understanding the relationships between the number of moles of a substance and the mass, volume or number of particles present in a sample of a substance will help in unit conversions when solving stoichiometry problems. How confident do you feel about calculating these relationships? Do you think you would award yourself full marks for the calculate questions in this section? If not, how could you improve your answers so you feel confident about your calculations?

5.3 Moles and solution chemistry

1   a   What equation is used to calculate the concentration of a solution?

   b   What are the units used to measure the concentration of a solution?

2   A solution containing ammonia requires 25.0 cm³ of 0.100 mol/dm³ hydrochloric acid to reach the equivalence point of a titration.

   a   Give a balanced symbol equation for the reaction of ammonia with hydrochloric acid.   [2]

   b   Calculate the number of moles of hydrochloric acid and ammonia that react.   [2]

   c   Calculate the mass of ammonia in the solution.   [2]

[Total: 6]

≪ RECALL AND CONNECT 2 ≪

Can you recall what a molecule is? Provide an example of a molecule.

3   Two salts can be made from titration reactions between potassium hydroxide and sulfuric acid. These are potassium sulfate, K_2SO_4 and potassium hydrogen sulfate, $KHSO_4$.

In a titration 25.0 cm³ of 2.53 mol/dm³ potassium hydroxide was neutralised by 28.2 cm³ of dilute sulfuric acid.

The equation for the reaction is:

$$2KOH(aq) + H_2SO_4(aq) \rightleftharpoons K_2SO_4(aq) + 2H_2O(l)$$

Calculate the concentration of the sulfuric acid used:

a   per number of moles of KOH used   [1]
b   per number of moles of H_2SO_4 needed to neutralise the KOH   [1]
c   as concentration of dilute sulfuric acid (mol/dm³).   [1]

[Total: 3]

4   Calculate the mass of sodium hydroxide required to make 500 cm³ of a solution with a concentration of 0.10 mol/dm³ aqueous sodium hydroxide.   **[Total: 4]**

UNDERSTAND THIS TERM

- titration

REFLECTION

How confident do you feel determining the concentration of a solution, given the number of moles and volume? Are there any strategies you can think of that would help you?

SELF-ASSESSMENT CHECKLIST

Let's revisit the Knowledge focus and Exam skills focus for this chapter.

Decide how confident you are with each statement.

Now I can:	Show it	Needs more work	Almost there	Confident to move on
establish how the mole is the unit of amount of a substance in chemistry	Calculate the number of particles, mass or volume of a substance given the number of moles.			
calculate empirical and molecular formulae using appropriate data and the concept of the mole	Deduce the empirical and molecular formula of a compound given the percentage masses.			

CONTINUED

Now I can:	Show it	Needs more work	Almost there	Confident to move on
calculate the relationship between the number of moles of a substance and the mass or number of particles present	Calculate the relationship between the number of moles of a substance and the mass, volume or number of particles present in a sample of that substance.			
calculate reacting masses, limiting reactants and amount of product for a stated reaction	Write balanced symbol equations, deduce ratios of the compounds in the equation and complete mole calculations.			
calculate the percentage composition by mass of a compound, and the percentage yield and purity of a product of a given reaction	Calculate percentage composition, yield and purity given the actual and theoretical values.			
describe how the molar gas volume for any gas is 24 dm^3 at r.t.p. and use this value for calculations on reactions involving gases	Calculate volumes of gases formed or used in a chemical reaction involving gases.			
understand the different units used to express the concentration of a solution and use them when calculating the concentration of a solution from titration experiments	List the different types of units and know how to use them in calculations of solution concentrations from a given number of moles and volume.			
show that I understand the 'calculate' and 'show (that)' command words and answer 'calculate' and 'show (that)' questions.	Write your own 'calculate' question and ask a classmate to try it and then mark it and give them feedback. Do the same with a 'show (that)' question.			

6 Electrochemistry

The 'suggest' command word can be used in two different ways: there may be no definitive answer or you may need to draw upon wider knowledge to deal with an unfamiliar context. The latter usually requires you to use higher-order thinking skills such as analysis, critical thinking and problem-solving. You can prepare for challenging 'suggest' questions by working through past exam questions to enable you to understand unfamiliar chemistry and contexts.

Suggest	apply knowledge and understanding to situations where there are a range of valid responses in order to make proposals/put forward considerations.

6.1 Types of electrical conductivity

1   Which of the following materials conduct electricity as a solid?

aluminium	poly(styrene)	brass
diamond	graphite	copper
steel	poly(ethene)	gold
sulfur	silver	iodine

2   Draw a diagram to show how you could test the electrical conductivity of a liquid.

3   Explain the difference between metallic conductivity and conductivity through ionically bonded liquids and solids.   **[Total: 3]**

> ### UNDERSTAND THESE TERMS
> - electrical conductor
> - insulator
> - electrolysis
> - electrolyte
> - non-electrolytes
> - electrodes

≪ RECALL AND CONNECT 1 ≪

How do metal atoms and non-metal atoms form ions to make ionic compounds?

REFLECTION

How does your understanding of ionic bonding help you to understand and explain electrolysis?

> ### UNDERSTAND THESE TERMS
> - cathode
> - anode
> - electrolytic cell
> - cation
> - anion
> - decomposition

6.2 Products of electrolysis

1   Copy and complete the table to show the products formed at the anode and cathode when each of the following molten compounds are electrolysed.

Electrolyte	Product at cathode	Product at anode
potassium iodide		
copper(II) bromide		
aluminium oxide		

2   Electrolysis of sodium chloride can give different products at the electrodes depending on the conditions of the electrolyte. Copy and complete the table to show which products are formed under the different conditions described.

Electrolyte	Product at cathode	Product at anode
molten sodium chloride (NaCl(l))		
concentrated sodium chloride solution (NaCl(aq))		
dilute sodium chloride solution (NaCl(aq))		

3   Molten lead bromide is electrolysed.

a   Describe what you would observe at the cathode.   [1]

b   State which product would be formed at the cathode.   [1]

c   Give the ionic half-equation for the reaction happening at the cathode.   [2]

[Total: 4]

≪ RECALL AND CONNECT 2 ≪

Graphite is used to make electrodes for electrolysis because it conducts electricity and is inert. In terms of its structure and bonding, explain why graphite conducts electricity.

REFLECTION

'**Cat**s have **paws**' is one way that some students remember that **pos**itive ions are attracted to the **cat**hode. Is this a strategy that will work for you? Can you think of other words or sentences that would help you to remember concepts? If not, you could make up some of your own.

UNDERSTAND THESE TERMS

- half-equation
- electroplating
- quantitative

6.3 Hydrogen as a fuel

1   Why is hydrogen regarded as a non-polluting fuel?

2   Suggest **one** advantage and **one** disadvantage of using hydrogen as a fuel for motor vehicles.   **[Total: 2]**

UNDERSTAND THESE TERMS

- fuel cell
- fuel

SELF-ASSESSMENT CHECKLIST

Let's revisit the Knowledge focus and Exam skills focus for this chapter.

Decide how confident you are with each statement.

Now I can:	Show it	Needs more work	Almost there	Confident to move on
describe metals as electrical conductors and non-metallic materials as non-conducting insulators	Create a table with two columns labelled 'conductors' and 'insulators'. In each column, list five household items and the materials they are made from.			
define electrolysis and identify the components of an electrolytic cell	Draw a labelled diagram of an electrolytic cell and use it to explain how electrolysis works to a friend or family member.			
describe and predict the electrolysis products of binary compounds in the molten state	Make two sets of cards - one with names of metals and another with oxide/chloride/bromide/iodide. Play a game where you choose a card from each set at random and identify the products of electrolysis from the compound they make.			
describe the electrolysis of concentrated sodium chloride solution and dilute sulfuric acid using inert electrodes	Draw a labelled diagram of the Hofmann voltameter to electrolyse aqueous dilute sulfuric acid. Show how it would be different if concentrated sodium chloride solution were used instead.			
describe how to electroplate a metal object	Use cell diagrams and/or a Venn diagram to explain how a cell used for electroplating is different from one used for electrolysis.			
state that a hydrogen–oxygen fuel cell generates electricity	Say how a hydrogen fuel cell is different from burning hydrogen as a fuel.			

CONTINUED

Now I can:	Show it	Needs more work	Almost there	Confident to move on
predict the products of electrolysis of a halide compound in dilute and concentrated solutions	Add the options of (a) molten or (b) dilute aqueous or (c) concentrated aqueous to your revision cards with metals and halides. Or make separate cards for each. Add these options/cards as another layer to your game.			
describe how charge is transferred in electrolysis and learn how to construct ionic half-equations	Write the half-equations on the other side of your revision card game from earlier and when you predict the products, write the half-equations too.			
identify the products of the electrolysis of copper(II) sulfate solution using graphite or copper electrodes	Draw two electrolysis cells with copper sulfate as the electrolyte. Using carbon electrode on one and copper electrodes in the other, annotate each diagram to show the similarities and differences. Write the half-equations for the reactions that occur at each electrode.			
describe the advantages and disadvantages of hydrogen–oxygen fuel cells	Look at the table of advantages and disadvantages of using a hydrogen-oxygen fuel cell in your coursebook. Close your book and try to rewrite both lists. Check to make sure you have included all of the points. Repeat as necessary.			
show that I understand the 'suggest' command word and answer 'suggest' questions.	Explain to a friend how you would answer a 'suggest' questions.			

Exam practice 2

This section contains past paper questions from previous Cambridge exams, which draw together your knowledge on a range of topics that you have covered up to this point. These questions give you the opportunity to test your knowledge and understanding. Additional past paper practice questions can be found in the accompanying digital material.

The following question has an example student response and commentary provided. Once you have worked through the question, read the student response and commentary. Are your answers different to the sample answers?

1   Ammonia is manufactured by combining nitrogen and hydrogen at high temperature and pressure.

$$\text{nitrogen + hydrogen} \underset{}{\overset{\text{catalyst}}{\rightleftharpoons}} \text{ammonia}$$

   a   i   What is the meaning of the symbol $\rightleftharpoons$?   [1]

        ii   What is the purpose of the catalyst?   [1]

   b   The graph shows the percentage yield of ammonia at different temperatures.

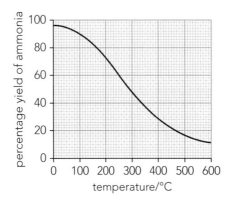

        i   Describe how the percentage yield of ammonia changes with temperature.   [1]

        ii   Deduce the percentage yield of ammonia at 400 °C.   [1]

c   Copper(II) oxide reacts with ammonia.

copper(II) oxide + ammonia → copper + nitrogen + water

When 20 g of copper(II) oxide react with an excess of ammonia,
16 g of copper are formed. Calculate the mass of copper formed
when 140 g of copper(II) oxide react with an excess of ammonia.   [1]

d   Ammonia is used in the manufacture of nylon.

Give **one** use of nylon.   [1]

[Total: 6]

Cambridge IGCSE Chemistry (0620) Paper 31, Q8 November 2017

Example student response			Commentary
1	a	i reversible	The student's response showed a good knowledge recall of the meaning of the symbol. *This answer is awarded 1 out of 1 mark.*
		ii speed up rate of reaction	The response here again showed a good knowledge recall of the purpose of a catalyst. *This answer is awarded 1 out of 1 mark.*
	b	i decrease	The response showed that the student was able to analyse the graph and is able to identify the pattern shown on the graph. However, the student has only given a one-word answer, 'decrease'. Giving only a one-word answer could be considered incorrect as the meaning is unclear. The word 'decrease' used here could mean that the percentage decreases as the temperature decreases, but this is incorrect. *This answer is awarded 0 out of 1 mark.*
		ii high	The student's response here showed a lack of understanding of the command term, 'deduce'. The student might not know what the question is asking for and/or understand the term 'deduce' as 'discuss' or 'write down'. *This answer is awarded 0 out of 1 mark.*
	c	20 g CuO : 16 g Cu 140 g CuO : ? g Cu 20 − 16 = 4 140 − 4 = 136 g	The response here demonstrated a lack of calculation skills and analytical skills. The student was not able to analyse the information given of how 20 g CuO would produce 16 g Cu instead subtracting 16 g Cu from 20 g CuO. *This answer is awarded 0 out of 1 mark.*
	d	fishing line	Here, the student's response showed a good knowledge recall of one use of nylon. *This answer is awarded 1 out of 1 mark.*

2   Now that you've read the commentary to the previous question, try to write a full
mark scheme for Question 1. This will check if you've understood exactly why
each mark has (or has not) been awarded.

The following question has an example student response and commentary provided. Once you have worked through the question, read the student response and commentary. Are your answers different to the sample answers?

3   Ethanol is manufactured from glucose, $C_6H_{12}O_6$, by fermentation according to the following equation.

$$C_6H_{12}O_6 \rightarrow 2C_2H_5OH + 2CO_2$$

In an experiment, 30.0 g of glucose was fermented.

a   Calculate the number of moles of glucose in 30.0 g.   [2]

b   Calculate the maximum mass of ethanol that could be obtained from 30.0 g of glucose.   [2]

c   Calculate the volume of carbon dioxide at room temperature and pressure that can be obtained from 30.0 g of glucose.   [1]

[Total: 5]

Cambridge IGCSE Chemistry (0620) Paper 32, Q7b March 2015

Example student response	Commentary
3 a $M_r\ C_6H_{12}O_6 = (12 \times 6) + 12 + (16 \times 6) = 180$ $n = m/M_r = \dfrac{30}{180} = 0.16$ mols	$\dfrac{1}{6}$ should be rounded to 0.167. *This answer is awarded 1 out of 2 marks.*
b $M_r\ C_2H_5OH = (12 \times 2) + 5 + 16 + 1$ $= 46$ g/mol $m = n \times M_r = 0.16 \times 46 = 7.36$ g	The student has not used the mole ratio from the equation to multiply by two to give the correct moles of ethanol formed. Allowing for this error, the working shows the correct calculation for mass given the number of moles used. *This answer is awarded 1 out of 2 marks.*
c volume $= 0.16 \times 24 = 3.84$ dm³	The student has used the molar volume of a gas, but again has not used the mole ratio from the equation to get the correct number of moles of CO_2 formed. *This answer is awarded 0 out of 1 mark.*

Now you have read the commentary to the previous question, here is a similar question which you should attempt. Use the information from the previous response and commentary to guide you as you answer the questions.

4   When hydrated magnesium sulfate crystals, $MgSO_4 \cdot xH_2O$, are heated they give off water.

$$MgSO_4 \cdot xH_2O(s) \rightarrow MgSO_4(s) + xH_2O(g)$$

A student carries out an experiment to determine the value of x in $MgSO_4 \cdot xH_2O$.

Step 1 Hydrated magnesium sulfate crystals were weighed.

Step 2 Hydrated magnesium sulfate crystals were heated.

Step 3 The remaining solid was weighed.

a   Describe how the student can ensure that all the water is given off.   [2]

b   In an experiment, all the water was removed from 1.23 g of $MgSO_4 \cdot xH_2O$.
The mass of $MgSO_4$ remaining was 0.60 g.

M_r: $MgSO_4 = 120$; M_r: $H_2O = 18$

Determine the value of x using the following steps:

- Calculate the number of moles of $MgSO_4$ remaining:

- Calculate the mass of H_2O given off.

mass of H_2O = ... g

- Calculate the moles of H_2O given off.

- Determine the value of x.   [4]

[Total: 6]

Cambridge IGCSE Chemistry (0620) Paper 43, Q4d November 2020

The following question has an example student response and commentary provided.

Once you have worked through the question, compare your answer to the student response and commentary.

5   Chemical reactions are always accompanied by an energy change.

Aluminium is extracted by the electrolysis of a molten mixture which contains aluminium oxide, Al_2O_3. This decomposes to form aluminium at the negative electrode and oxygen at the positive electrode.

a   Write an ionic equation for the reaction at the negative electrode.   [2]

b   Complete the ionic equation for the reaction at the positive electrode.

$2O^{2-} \rightarrow$ .... + ...   [2]

c   Is the reaction exothermic or endothermic? Explain your answer.   [1]

[Total: 5]

Cambridge IGCSE Chemistry (0620) Paper 33, Q6 June 2015

Example student response	Commentary
5 a $Al^{3+} + e^- \rightarrow Al_3$	The student has correctly identified the aluminium ion, but the electrons are not balanced, and aluminium does not form a triatomic molecule. *This answer is awarded 1 out of 2 marks.*
b $2O^{2-} \rightarrow 2O + 2e^-$	The formula for oxygen is incorrect and the equation is not balanced in terms of charge. *This answer is awarded 0 out of 2 marks.*
c The reaction is endothermic because energy had to be supplied to break up the compound.	Energy change identified and explained correctly. *This answer is awarded 1 out of 1 mark.*

Being asked to identify products at the electrodes in electrolysis of molten compounds is common in exams. The following question offers another situation for you to apply your understanding.

6   a   Molten lead(II) bromide can be electrolysed using the apparatus shown.

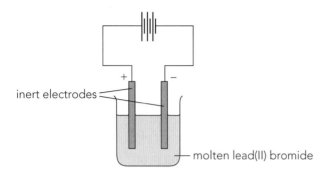

inert electrodes

molten lead(II) bromide

The negative electrode is called the cathode.

State the name of the positive electrode.   [1]

   b   Predict the products of the electrolysis of molten lead(II) bromide at:

the negative electrode

the positive electrode.   [2]

[Total: 3]

Cambridge IGCSE Chemistry (0620) Paper 33, Q5a, b June 2018

7 Chemical energetics

An important part of providing appropriate responses is to prioritise and manage time in answering questions of varying lengths and details. In this chapter you will practise different question types and become aware of how the marks are distributed throughout the paper. For the longer questions, you should plan your response before writing it. This should help you to recognise where more time should be spent.

Making connections between concepts is also important. To answer calculation exam questions effectively, you must be able to recall and apply knowledge.

Question 1c in Exam practice 3 provides further practice of calculation questions to show your working and apply the concept learnt.

Working out for calculations can draw out connections in the knowledge required.

7.1 Physical and chemical changes

1   There are two types of changes known as physical changes and chemical changes. Produce a table with two columns and categorise each of the following examples as physical changes or chemical changes.

> frying an egg   neutralisation of hydrochloric acid   boiling of water
> freezing of water   rusting of iron   dissolving salt in water

2   Copy the text below and fill in the blanks using the words provided.

> chemical change   physical change   new
> reversible   irreversible   chemically

An example of a ……………….......... occurs when ice melts to become liquid water. This is an example of a/an ……………….......... process because no ………………. substances are formed and the substance remains ……………….......... unchanged.

Magnesium burning in oxygen is an example of a …………………........... The product formed in this process is magnesium oxide, which is different to the reactants. This is an example of a/an ………………........................ process.

3   Describe the similarities and differences between physical changes and chemical changes.

[Total: 2]

> **UNDERSTAND THESE TERMS**
>
> • chemical reaction (change)
>
> • physical change

≪ RECALL AND CONNECT 1 ≪

The products formed in a chemical change cannot be separated from the reaction mixture using physical methods. What method should be used to separate lead and bromine from the compound lead(II) bromide?

7.2 Exothermic and endothermic reactions

1   Figure 7.1 is a reaction pathway diagram showing the change in enthalpy during chemical reactions.

a   Copy and complete Figure 7.1 to produce a reaction pathway diagram for the exothermic reaction between methane and oxygen to produce carbon dioxide and water by adding arrows showing the enthalpy change and labels. Your labels should include short descriptions stating:

   • heat released/heat absorbed

   • reactants

   • products.

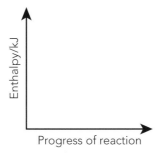

Figure 7.1: Reaction pathway diagram for the reaction between methane and oxygen

b   Draw a reaction pathway diagram for an endothermic reaction by adding arrows showing the enthalpy change and labels. Your labels should include short descriptions stating:

   • heat released/heat absorbed

   • reactants

   • products.

2   Ethane, C_2H_6, reacts with oxygen to form carbon dioxide and water. This is a type of combustion which can be represented by the balanced symbol equation:

$$2C_2H_6 + 7O_2 \rightarrow 4CO_2 + 6H_2O$$

a   State whether this is an endothermic or exothermic reaction.   [1]

b   Explain your answer to part **a** in terms of bond breaking, bond formation and enthalpy change, ΔH.   [2]

[Total: 3]

3 The reaction between nitrogen and oxygen forms nitrogen monoxide.
The balanced symbol equation for this reaction is:

$$N_2(g) + O_2(g) \rightarrow 2NO(g)$$

Bond	Bond energy kJ/mol
O = O	495
N = O	607
N ≡ N	941

Use the bond energies in the table to calculate the enthalpy change,
in kJ/mol. Show your working.   **[Total: 3]**

≪ RECALL AND CONNECT 2 ≪

There are many examples of endothermic and exothermic processes that we
use daily. For example, combustion reactions are used to generate electricity
in power stations. Is combustion an example of an endothermic or exothermic
change? Give reasons.

UNDERSTAND THESE TERMS

- activation energy (E_a)
- bond energy
- enthalpy (H)
- enthalpy change (ΔH)
- reaction pathway diagram (energy level diagram)

REFLECTION

Were you able to make the connections between concepts and apply them
to the calculation question in this section?

Try writing down what you will do to strengthen your learning for these areas.
For example, make a table to categorise the differences between endothermic
and exothermic reactions which includes the reaction pathway diagrams.

How will you check that you have improved your understanding? Check with
your peers or speak to a teacher if you are confused about the difference
between bonds breaking and bonds forming and see if there are more
questions for you to practise.

SELF-ASSESSMENT CHECKLIST

Let's revisit the Knowledge focus and Exam skills focus for this chapter.

Decide how confident you are with each statement.

Now I can:	Show it	Needs more work	Almost there	Confident to move on
identify and understand the differences between physical and chemical changes	Compare and contrast the different properties of physical and chemical changes.			

CONTINUED

Now I can:	Show it	Needs more work	Almost there	Confident to move on
see how some chemical reactions and physical changes are exothermic while others are endothermic	List examples of physical and chemical changes and identify which ones are exothermic and which ones are endothermic.			
define exothermic and endothermic reactions in terms of thermal energy transfer	Define exothermic and endothermic processes using ideas about thermal energy.			
interpret reaction pathway diagrams for exothermic and endothermic reactions	Draw labelled reaction pathway diagrams to distinguish between exothermic and endothermic processes.			
understand that for an exothermic reaction the enthalpy change (ΔH) is negative and for an endothermic reaction the enthalpy change (ΔH) is positive	Make a table to compare exothermic and endothermic reactions in terms of enthalpy changes.			
state that bond breaking is endothermic and bond making is exothermic, and use these ideas to calculate ΔH for a reaction	Practise calculation questions and show working on how to calculate bond breaking, bond forming and total enthalpy change.			
make connections between concepts by showing working for calculation questions.	Analyse the values obtained from the calculation question on bond breaking and bond forming and the +/− sign for the final answer and draw conclusions about whether the reaction is endothermic or exothermic.			

8 Rates of reaction

Sometimes you can understand the chemistry and write an answer that is correct, but it does not manage to meet the criteria in the marksheme. You might, for example, state something that you see on a graph when you were asked to explain something. Or you may spend time providing numerous advantages and disadvantages when the question only asked for two advantages. Always read the question carefully; take note of the command word(s) and the number of marks available.

8.1 Factors affecting the rate of reaction

1 List three factors that can affect the rate of reaction.
Describe the effect of each one.

2 How can each of the following be changed?

a surface area of a solid

b concentration of a solution

c pressure of a gas

UNDERSTAND THESE TERMS
• catalyst
• enzymes
• reaction rate

3 Some students measured the volume of hydrogen produced in the reaction between magnesium and (excess) hydrochloric acid at two different concentrations. Figure 8.1 shows the graph they plotted of the volume produced (cm^3) against time (s):

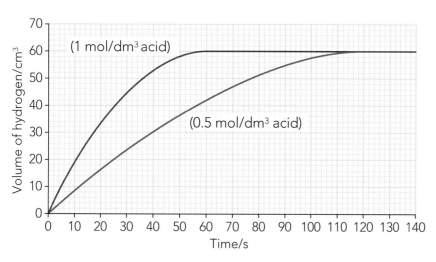

Figure 8.1

a Evaluate the rate of the reaction at the different concentrations shown on the graph. [2]

b Explain why the volume of hydrogen stops changing when it reaches 60 cm^3. [2]

[Total: 4]

8.2 Collision theory of reaction rate

1 What is the connection between particles colliding, the energy of the particles and reaction rate?

2   Use the collision theory to explain the effect of each of the following factors on the rate of reaction between calcium carbonate and hydrochloric acid:

   a   surface area of the calcium carbonate

   b   concentration of the hydrochloric acid

   c   temperature of the acid.

3   Figure 8.2 shows the reaction pathway diagram for an exothermic reaction.

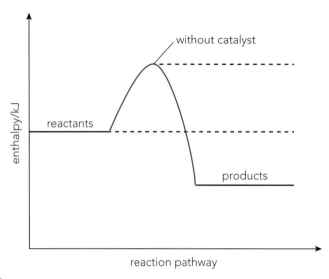

Figure 8.2

UNDERSTAND THESE TERMS

- adsorption
- collision theory

   a   On a copy of the diagram, sketch arrows and label E_a – the activation energy and ΔH – the enthalpy of the reaction.   [1]

   b   On your copy of the diagram, sketch and label a curve to show how a catalyst affects the reaction pathway.   [2]

   c   Give two advantages of using a catalyst to make chemical products.   [2]

[Total: 5]

« RECALL AND CONNECT 1 «

1   Draw the reaction pathway diagram for an endothermic reaction.

2   Label the activation energy and enthalpy of a reaction and sketch what you would expect the reaction pathway to look like when a catalyst is used.

REFLECTION

Information about reaction rate can be obtained by measuring the *reduction in mass of a reactant or the formation of a product* over time. The reaction can be *monitored continuously.* Are you confident you could categorise the reactions and experiments in this chapter according to both these criteria? If you were to switch either category for any of the reactions, think how you would go about measuring it.

SELF-ASSESSMENT CHECKLIST

Let's revisit the Knowledge focus and Exam skills focus for this chapter.

Decide how confident you are with each statement.

Now I can:	Show it	Needs more work	Almost there	Confident to move on
describe the effects of various factors on the rate of a chemical reaction	Demonstrate how the factors affect rate on a revision card by using arrows to indicate the effect: (e.g. temperature ↑ = rate ↑)			
describe how a catalyst increases the rate of a reaction and is unchanged at the end of that reaction	Make a word cloud with catalyst at the centre and other key words needed to explain its meaning.			
describe how to investigate the rates of various different reactions	Look through your notes or coursebook to find how you can measure the rate of reaction for the different reactions you have learned about. Draw labelled diagrams for each reaction from memory, and check your diagrams. Correct or add anything as needed.			
evaluate different practical methods for investigating the rate of a reaction	Evaluate each of your labelled diagrams on the rate experiments by making a list beside each one of what did and didn't work well, and other reactions you could use that method to measure the rate for.			
describe collision theory	Describe collision theory to a family member or friend. Answer their questions about it.			
explain the effects of various factors on reaction rate using collision theory	Draw annotated diagrams to show how collision theory explains how rate of the reaction changes when we change various factors.			

CONTINUED

Now I can:	Show it	Needs more work	Almost there	Confident to move on
explain how an increase in temperature produces an increase in reaction rate	Write a paragraph to explain how increasing the temperature of a reaction does more than increase the frequency of collisions. What 'more' does it do and how does the more contribute to the increase in the rate?			
discuss the role of a catalyst in increasing reaction rate	Add key words to explain how a catalyst works to your word cloud.			
carefully read questions and available marks to help structure my answer.	Look through this chapter – or any other chapter – and highlight the command words and available marks. What does this information tell you about the answer you need to provide?			

9 Reversible reactions and equilibrium

KNOWLEDGE FOCUS

In this chapter you will answer questions on:

- reversible reactions
- Haber process and Contact process
- fertilisers.

EXAM SKILLS FOCUS

In this chapter you will:

- show that you understand the 'predict' command word and can answer 'predict' questions.

'Predict' questions require you to outline possible outcomes based on data or information given to you in the question, which may need to be combined with your own knowledge and understanding. When asked to make a prediction, you are expected to suggest what may happen based on available evidence. To answer the question successfully you will need to use all the information you have been given in your answer.

| Predict | suggest what may happen based on available information. |

9.1 Reversible reactions

1 Write down the symbol that is used to indicate that a reaction is reversible.

2 Name two hydrated salts that can be used to test for the presence of water and describe the colour change that occurs in each one when it changes from the anhydrous (dehydrated) form to the hydrated form.

3 The forward reaction in the production of ammonia from nitrogen and hydrogen in the Haber process is exothermic:

$$N_2(g) + 3H_2(g) \rightleftharpoons 2NH_3(g)$$

Predict what will happen to the position of equilibrium and the yield of ammonia produced when:

a   the temperature is increased   [1]

b   the pressure is increased   [1]

c   the ammonia is removed as soon as it is formed   [1]

d   an iron catalyst is added.   [1]

[Total: 4]

« RECALL AND CONNECT 1 «

How does increasing the temperature and using a catalyst, either individually or at the same time, affect the rate of a reaction?

REFLECTION

How did you find the 'predict' question in this section? Check your answer against the one provided. Were you able to use the information available to correctly suggest what may happen?

9.2 Haber process and Contact process

1 Write down the reaction equations and conditions for:

a   the Haber process

b   the Contact process.

2 In what two ways is the sulfur dioxide needed for the Contact process obtained?

UNDERSTAND THESE TERMS

- Contact process
- Haber process

3 Explain why the pressures used in the Haber process and the Contact process are higher than atmospheric pressure. **[Total: 3]**

<< RECALL AND CONNECT 2 <<

Explain why a temperature of 450 °C and an iron catalyst are used for the Haber process.

REFLECTION

Processes describe changes with a beginning, a middle and an end.

How can you represent the Haber process and the Contact process in such a way that you show the changes step-by-step?

UNDERSTAND THESE TERMS

- compromise temperature
- desulfurisation
- fertiliser

9.3 Fertilisers

1 What are the three important elements provided by NPK fertilisers and why do plants need them?

2 Why is solubility important when considering the use of salts as fertilisers?

3 Calculate the percentage by mass of nitrogen in ammonium nitrate and therefore the mass of nitrogen contained in a 50 kg bag of ammonium nitrate fertiliser. **[Total: 2]**

UNDERSTAND THESE TERMS

- compound fertiliser
- NPK fertiliser

<< RECALL AND CONNECT 3 <<

Calculate the relative formula mass of ammonium nitrate (NH_4NO_3).

Relative atomic masses:

N = 14 g/mol   H = 1 g/mol   O = 16 g/mol

SELF-ASSESSMENT CHECKLIST

Let's revisit the Knowledge focus and Exam skills focus for this chapter.

Decide how confident you are with each statement.

Now I can:	Show it	Needs more work	Almost there	Confident to move on
understand that some chemical reactions are reversible	Write down some examples of reversible reactions, using equations and the symbol for a reversible reaction.			
describe how changing conditions can alter the direction of a reversible reaction	Draw a labelled diagram of the experiment to show the reversible reaction between hydrated and anhydrous copper sulfate.			
describe the use of reversible reactions as a chemical test for the presence of water	Explain how you can use anhydrous cobalt chloride or anhydrous copper sulfate as a test for water.			
state that ammonium salts and nitrates can be used as fertilisers	Write down the names and formulae of two ammonium salts that are used as fertilisers.			
describe the use of NPK fertilisers for improved plant growth	Draw a diagram of a plant. Name and label the different parts of the plant that benefit from nitrogen, phosphorous and potassium and describe how the plant obtains these nutrients from the soil that have been treated with NPK fertilisers.			
state that in a closed system a reversible reaction can reach an equilibrium where the rate of the forward reaction is equal to the rate of the reverse reaction	Draw a diagram of a closed and an open system containing nitrogen, hydrogen and ammonia and use it to explain why equilibrium is reached in a closed system but not in an open system.			

CONTINUED

Now I can:	Show it	Needs more work	Almost there	Confident to move on
predict and explain how the position of an equilibrium is affected by various changes in the conditions	Make a table summarising what happens to the position of equilibrium for the exothermic reaction between sulfur dioxide and oxygen to produce sulfur trioxide when you increase or decrease the temperature, pressure and carry out the reaction with and without a catalyst.			
state the symbol equations for the reversible reactions used to produce ammonia in the Haber process and sulfuric acid in the Contact process and give the sources of the reactants for these two processes	Make a flow diagram for each of the Haber process and the Contact process, using as few words as necessary for each step, stating the raw materials of each and writing the symbol equations.			
outline the typical conditions used in the Haber and Contact processes	Add the conditions to your flow diagrams in the previous step if you have not already done so.			
understand the 'predict' command word and answer 'predict' questions.	Say what the command word 'predict' means. After you have answered 'predict' questions in this chapter, explain why this command word was chosen for that question.			

10 Redox reactions

The 'state' command word is often used for short answer questions.

State	express in clear terms.

It is important not to provide too much information or detail when you answer 'state' questions. You are not expected to provide detailed explanations or descriptions. 'State' is often combined with another command word, such as 'explain' or 'suggest'. When you come across questions with two command words, make sure your answer addresses both.

10.1 Combustion, oxidation and reduction

1 Copy and complete the following table by identifying the oxidising agent and reducing agent in each reaction.

Reactions	Oxidising agent	Reducing agent
$Fe_2O_3(s) + 3CO(g) \rightarrow 2Fe(s) + 3CO_2(g)$		
$CuO(s) + H_2(g) \rightarrow Cu(s) + H_2O(l)$		
$ZnO(s) + C(s) \rightarrow Zn(s) + CO(g)$		
$Mg(s) + CuO(s) \rightarrow Cu(s) + MgO(s)$		

2 Copy and complete the sentences. Fill in the blanks about corrosion with the following words.

> redox   oxidation   electrons
>
> reduction   air   iron(III) oxide

Corrosion occurs when a metal's surface reacts with ………………., water or

other substances. Corrosion is a type of ……………… reaction as it involves

both oxidation and ……………… .

In corrosion, iron undergoes ……………… when it reacts with oxygen to form

rust, also known as ……………… .

Oxygen accepts ……………… from iron in the process of reduction.

3 Define the terms *oxidation* and *reduction*.

[Total: 2]

≪ RECALL AND CONNECT 1 ≪

In the Contact process, sulfuric acid is manufactured from sulfur dioxide and oxygen. A redox reaction takes place when oxygen is reacted with sulfur dioxide to produce sulfur trioxide shown in the equation:

$$2SO_2(g) + O_2(g) \rightleftharpoons 2SO_3(g)$$

Describe how an increase in the concentration of the product, sulfur trioxide, will affect the position of the equilibrium.

UNDERSTAND THESE TERMS

- combustion
- corrosion
- oxidation
- oxidising agent
- rancid
- redox reaction
- reduction
- reducing agent
- respiration

10.2 Redox reactions

1 The table shows a range of oxidation numbers. Copy and complete the table by placing the symbols of the elements provided in the box next to their correct oxidation numbers. Each element may be used once, more than once or not at all. There may be more than one element for some oxidation numbers.

Na^+	Cl^-	N^{3-}	O^{2-}	S^{2-}	Cu^{2+}
Cl_2	Fe^{3+}	H_2	Mg^{2+}	Al^{3+}	O_2

Oxidation numbers	Element(s)
+3	
+2	
+1	
0	
−1	
−2	
−3	

2 For each of the following questions, choose the correct element or compound from the list provided.

NiO	Mg	$Ni(NO_3)_2$	Cu_2O	Zn
$CuCO_3$	Al	Cr_2O_3	$Cr_2(SO_4)_3$	O_2

a State the element with an oxidation state of −2. [1]

b State **one** element with an oxidation state of +3. [1]

c State the two compounds that contain the same transition element in two different oxidation states. Justify your answer. [3]

[Total: 5]

3 The reaction between aqueous bromine and aqueous potassium iodide forms aqueous potassium bromide and iodine in a halogen displacement reaction.

State and explain the colour change you would observe. **[Total: 2]**

UNDERSTAND THESE TERMS

- displacement reaction
- oxidation number
- transition metals (transition elements)

≪ RECALL AND CONNECT 2 ≪

In the Haber process, ammonia is manufactured from nitrogen (N_2) and hydrogen (H_2). How are the gases nitrogen and hydrogen obtained for use in the Haber process?

REFLECTION

Which areas in this chapter were your strengths in and which do you need more practice in? For example, compare oxidation and reduction and summarise the differences, which include oxidising and reducing agents. How will you check that you have improved your understanding of these concepts? For example, could you identify the oxidation number of a specific element?

SELF-ASSESSMENT CHECKLIST

Let's revisit the Knowledge focus and Exam skills focus for this chapter.

Decide how confident you are with each statement.

Now I can:	Show it	Needs more work	Almost there	Confident to move on
describe how combustion reactions involve oxidation and reduction (redox) reactions	Describe the oxidation and reduction reactions taking place in combustion.			
define oxidation as the gain of oxygen and reduction as the loss of oxygen	Make a table to compare oxidation and reduction.			
use Roman numerals to indicate oxidation number	Write a list of the elements/ions/compounds with different oxidation numbers.			
define oxidation and reduction in terms of loss and gain of electrons	Make a table to compare oxidation and reduction.			
define the terms oxidising agent and reducing agent	Write down the meaning of the terms oxidising agent and reducing agent with examples.			
identify oxidation/oxidising agents and reduction/reducing agents in redox reactions	Practise identifying the oxidising agent and reducing agent, and examples of oxidation and reduction in given examples of redox reactions.			

CONTINUED

Now I can:	Show it	Needs more work	Almost there	Confident to move on
understand oxidation numbers, and define oxidation and reduction in terms of an increase and decrease in oxidation number	Practise recall of oxidation numbers of different elements in a compound in given examples of redox reactions.			
use oxidation numbers to identify oxidation/oxidising agents and reduction/ reducing agents	Make a list of oxidation numbers of different elements in a compound in given examples of redox reactions.			
describe the use of colour to identify oxidising or reducing agents and redox reactions	Create a table to memorise examples of oxidising and reducing agents, along with the use of colour and colour changes for each of these solutions.			
understand the command word 'state' and recognise that it is sometimes combined with another command word.	Write a 'state' question and mark scheme which combines 'state' with another command word. Ask a classmate to try to answer it.			

Exam practice 3

This section contains past paper questions from previous Cambridge exams, which draw together your knowledge on a range of topics that you have covered up to this point. These questions give you the opportunity to test your knowledge and understanding. Additional past paper practice questions can be found in the accompanying digital material.

The following question has an example student response and commentary provided. Once you have worked through the question, read the student response and commentary. Are your answers different to the sample answers?

1   This question is about phosphorus and compounds of phosphorus.

    a   A phosphorus molecule contains four phosphorus atoms **only**.
       What is the formula of a phosphorus molecule?   [1]

    b   Phosphorus reacts with chlorine gas to produce phosphorus(III) chloride, PCl_3.

        i   Write a symbol equation for the reaction between phosphorus and chlorine to produce phosphorus(III) chloride, PCl_3.   [2]

        ii Complete the dot-and-cross diagram to show the electron arrangement in a molecule of phosphorus(III) chloride, PCl_3. Show outer shell electrons only.   [2]

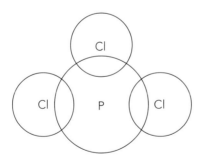

    c   Gaseous phosphorus(III) chloride, PCl_3, reacts with gaseous chlorine to form gaseous phosphorus(V) chloride, PCl_5.

$$PCl_3(g) + Cl_2(g) \rightarrow PCl_5(g)$$

       The chemical equation for this reaction can be represented as shown.

    i   Use the bond energies in the table to calculate the energy change, in kJ/mol, of the reaction.

bond	bond energy in kJ/mol
P–Cl	326
Cl–Cl	243

Energy needed to break bonds. .... kJ

Energy released when bonds are formed. .... kJ

Energy change of reaction. .... kJ/mol

[3]

    ii   Deduce whether the energy change for this reaction is exothermic or endothermic. Explain your answer. [1]

    iii Under certain conditions the reaction reaches equilibrium.

$$PCl_3(g) + Cl_2(g) \rightleftharpoons PCl_5(g)$$

State and explain the effect, if any, on the **position of equilibrium** if the pressure is increased. All other conditions are unchanged. [2]

d Phosphine, PH_3, is produced by the reaction between water and calcium phosphide, Ca_3P_2. Balance the chemical equation for this reaction.

$$Ca_3P_2 + ...H_2O ....Ca(OH)_2 + ...PH_3$$

[2]

e The phosphonium ion, PH_4^+, is similar to the ammonium ion.

    i   State the formula of the ammonium ion. [1]

    ii   Suggest the formula of phosphonium iodide. [1]

f Calcium phosphate contains the phosphate ion, PO_4^{3-}.

What is the formula of calcium phosphate? [1]

g Phosphorus forms another compound with hydrogen with the following composition by mass: P, 93.94%; H, 6.06%.

    i   Calculate the empirical formula of the compound [2]

    ii   The compound has a relative molecular mass of 66.

Deduce the molecular formula of the compound. [1]

[Total: 19]

Cambridge IGCSE Chemistry (0620) Paper 43, Q4 November 2019

Example student response	Commentary
1 a P_2	The student has shown that they understand that for a molecule, there should be more than one atom by using a subscript of '2'. However, this question has provided information that shows the molecule should consist of four phosphorus atoms only. Some students might be unfamiliar with seeing P_4 as a molecule or even using a subscript of '4' to represent a molecule. *This answer scores 0 out of 1 mark.*
b i $4P + 3Cl \rightarrow 4PCl_3$	The student has given the formula of chlorine as a single chlorine atom, Cl. This is a mistake commonly made by students when they see phosphorus react with chlorine as they tend to forget that the chlorine has to be in molecule state (Cl_2) and that the phosphorus also has to be in molecule state even though it is not being mentioned. The equation is unbalanced. Zero marks are awarded because the equation has to be balanced and accompanied with the correct formula to gain the marks. *This answer scores 0 out of 2 marks.*
ii	The student demonstrated good skills in completing the dot-and-cross diagram by making sure both chlorine and phosphorus meet the stable electron configuration. Therefore, both marks are awarded for showing six non-bonding electrons on three chlorine atoms and the shared bonding electrons. *This answer scores 2 out of 2 marks.*
c i bond breaking $= (326 \times 3) + (243 \times 1)$ $= 1221$ kJ bond forming $= (326 \times 5)$ $= 1630$ kJ Energy change $= 1630 - 1221$ $= 409$ kJ/mol	The student demonstrated a good basic understanding of how to calculate bond energies using the given structural diagram. Hence, two marks are awarded for getting the correct values for both bond breaking and bond forming. However, a common misconception here is to take the larger value and subtract the smaller value. Hence, neglecting the negative sign, which is essential in energy change. *This answer scores 2 out of 3 marks.*
ii Exothermic. More energy is released during bond forming than bond breaking.	This answer is incorrect. The correct answer should be endothermic. *This answer scores 0 out of 1 mark.*

Example student response	Commentary
iii Equilibrium remains constant because there are similar number of atoms in both reactants and products.	The response shows poor understanding of the topic chemical equilibria. Based on the symbol equation, the student needs to understand that the equilibrium will shift towards the side of the equation that has fewer gaseous molecules. In this case, there is only one molecule in the product side compared to two molecules on the reactant side. *This answer scores 0 out of 2 marks.*
d $Ca_3P_2 + 6H_2O \rightarrow 3Ca(OH)_2 + 2PH_3$	The student demonstrates good skills in balancing the equation. The numbers are correct and the equation is fully balanced. *This answer scores 2 out of 2 marks.*
e i NH_4^+	The response showed that the student was able to recall that the ammonium ion consists of both the elements nitrogen and hydrogen. The student was able to apply that to the given information about the phosphonium ion. *This answer scores 1 out of 1 mark.*
ii PHI_4	This demonstrates a common misconception among students when writing a chemical formula. Students tend to swap the subscript numbers around assuming that these numbers are part of the charge. In this response the student may have assumed that the PH_4 ion has a +4 charge and therefore assumed that four I⁻ ions are needed to balanced the charges. *This answer scores 0 out of 1 mark.*
f Ca_3PO_{42}	Another common mistake made by students is not including the brackets when swapping ion charges. *This answer scores 0 out of 1 mark.*
g i 93.94/31 and 6.06/1 = 3.03 and 6.06 = 1 : 2 ratio = PH_2	The response clearly shows mastery of the calculation of empirical formula. The student recalls that they need to divide the mass percentage by the molecular mass and then divide it by the smallest value to obtain the ratio. *This answer scores 2 out of 2 marks.*
ii $(PH_2)x = 66$ $(31 + (1 \times 2))x = 66$ $(31 + 2)x = 66$ $33x = 66$ $x = 66/33$ $x = 2$	The response shows that the student was able to calculate molecular formula. However, a common mistake is missing out the final stage of multiplying the 'x' number into the empirical formula to obtain the final molecular formula. *This answer scores 0 out of 1 mark.*

2 Now write an improved answer to the parts of Question 1 where you lost marks.
   Use the commentary to support you as you write your improved answers.

The following question has an example student response and commentary provided. Once you have worked through the question, compare your answer to the student response and commentary.

3 The equation for the reaction between sodium thiosulfate and hydrochloric acid is given below.

$$Na_2S_2O_3(aq) + 2HCl(aq) \rightarrow 2NaCl(aq) + S(s) + SO_2(g) + H_2O(l)$$

The speed of this reaction was investigated using the following experiment. A beaker containing 50 cm³ of 0.2 mol/dm³ sodium thiosulfate was placed on a black cross. 50 cm³ of 2.0 mol/dm³ hydrochloric acid was added and the clock was started.

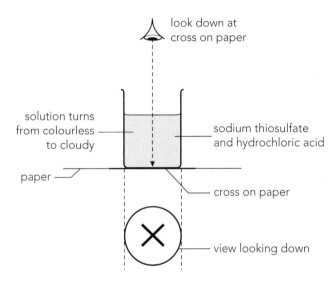

Initially the cross was clearly visible. When the solution became cloudy and the cross could no longer be seen, the clock was stopped and the time was recorded.

a The experiment was repeated with 25 cm³ of 0.2 mol/dm³ sodium thiosulfate and 25 cm³ of water. Typical results for this experiment and a further two experiments are given in the table.

experiment	1	2	3	4
volume of thiosulfate/cm³	50	40	25	10
volume of water/cm³	0	10	25	40
volume of acid/cm³	5	5	5	5
total volume/cm³	55	55	55	55
time/s	48	60	96	....

i Explain why it is necessary to keep the total volume the same in all the experiments. [2]

ii Complete the table. [1]

iii How and why does the speed of the reaction vary from experiment 1 to 4? [3]

b   The idea of collisions between reacting particles is used to explain changes in the speed of reactions. Use this idea to explain the following results.

volume of sodium thiosulfate/cm³	25	25
volume of water/cm³	25	25
volume of acid/cm³	5	5
temperature/°C	20	42
time/s	96	40

[4]

[Total: 10]

Cambridge IGCSE Chemistry (0620) Paper 32, Q3 June 2011

Example student response	Commentary
3 **a** **i** to make it a fair test	Specific reference needs to be made to the concentrations of thiosulfate (proportional to the volume added) and/or hydrochloric acid (keeps it the same) in the reaction mixtures. *This answer is awarded 1 out of 2 marks.*
ii 240s	Correct answer. Experiments 1 and 3 show that halving the concentration doubles the time taken. Experiment 4 is a quarter the concentrations of experiment 2, so the time taken will be four times as long. *This answer is awarded 1 out of 1 mark.*
iii The reaction is getting slower because the concentration of thiosulfate is decreasing. This is because there are less frequent collisions.	Correct answer. The student has stated explicitly what has happened to the rate of the reaction, described the change in the variable that has produced it, explained why correctly and included a reference to time. *This answer is awarded 3 out of 3 marks.*
b The reaction is faster at the higher temperature. This is because particles have more energy and there are more frequent collisions and a higher proportion of them have the activation energy.	Excellent answer. The student has stated explicitly what has happened to the speed/rate of the reaction, described the change in the variable that has produced it and explained why correctly, beyond the level of just 'more' collisions. *This answer is awarded 4 out of 4 marks.*

Now try this similar question. If you need support, use the commentary for the previous questions to guide you as you answer the questions.

4   A piece of magnesium was added to 100 cm^3 of an aqueous acid. The time taken for the metal to react completely was measured. This experiment was repeated using different aqueous acids. The same volume of acid was used in each experiment and the pieces of magnesium used were identical. In one experiment the reaction was carried out at a different temperature.

experiment	acid	concentration in mol/dm³	temperature/°C	time/minutes
A	propanoic	1.0	20	5
B	propanoic	1.0	30	3
C	propanoic	0.5	20	8
D	hydrochloric	1.0	20	1

Explain the following in terms of collision rate between reacting particles.

a   Why is the rate in experiment **C** slower than the rate in experiment **A**?   [2]

b   Why is the rate in experiment **B** faster than the rate in experiment **A**?   [2]

c   Why is the rate in experiment **D** faster than the rate in experiment **A**?   [3]

[Total: 7]

Cambridge IGCSE Chemistry (0620) Paper 32, Q4d June 2014

The following question has an example student response and commentary provided. Once you have worked through the question, compare your answer to the student response and commentary.

5   a   Nitrogen can be converted into ammonia by the Haber process.

Give the essential reaction conditions and write a chemical equation for the reaction occurring in the Haber process.

chemical equation:

reaction conditions: [5]

b   Some of the ammonia made by the Haber process is converted into nitric acid.

The first stage of this process is the oxidation of ammonia to make nitrogen monoxide.

$$4NH_3(g) + 5O_2(g) \rightleftharpoons 4NO(g) + 6H_2O(g)$$

The process is carried out at 900 °C and a pressure of 5 atmospheres using an alloy of platinum and rhodium as a catalyst.

The forward reaction is exothermic.

i   State the meaning of the term *catalyst*.   [2]

ii   State the meaning of the term *oxidation*.   [1]

iii Complete the table using the words **increase**, **decrease** or **no change**.

	effect on the rate of the forward reaction	effect on the equilibrium yield of NO(g)
increasing the temperature		
increasing the pressure		

[4]

[Total: 12]

Cambridge IGCSE Chemistry (0620) Paper 43, Q3b ii, c November 2020

Example student response	Commentary
5 a chemical equation: $N_2(g) + 3H_2(g) \rightleftharpoons 2NH_3(g)$ Reaction conditions: temperature of 450 °C, pressure of 200 atmospheres and an iron catalyst	All the reaction conditions given are correctly. Using the sign for a reversible reaction is important or stating it explicitly. Pressure can also be given as 20 000 kPa. Iron and catalyst must both be stated. *This answer is awarded 4 out of 4 marks.*
b i A catalyst increases the rate of a reaction.	Answer gets the first mark but is not sufficient for both. The student should state that the catalyst is not used up in the reaction or that it lowers the activation energy. *This answer is awarded 1 out of 2 marks.*
ii reaction with oxygen	Answer is not incorrect but falls short of the mark. Gain of oxygen should be stated explicitly. *This answer is awarded 0 out of 1 mark.*
iii <table><tr><td></td><td>Effect on the rate of the forword reaction</td><td>Effect on the equilibrium yield of NO(g)</td></tr><tr><td>increasing the temperature</td><td>increases</td><td>increases</td></tr><tr><td>increasing the pressure</td><td>increases</td><td>increases</td></tr></table>	Increasing the temperature and the pressure both increase the rate of the forward reaction, since there will be more frequent collisions for both changes. The effect on equilibrium is incorrect. Questions on rate and equilibrium are challenging since the effect on rate can be different from the effect on yield. *This answer is awarded 2 out of 4 marks.*

Having looked at the commentary to the previous question, especially on the more challenging aspects of explaining the Haber process, try this question to help you practise your own response.

6 Ammonia is manufactured by the Haber process. Nitrogen and hydrogen are passed over a catalyst at a temperature of 450 °C and a pressure of 200 atmospheres.

The equation for the reaction is as follows.

$$N_2 + 3H_2 \rightleftharpoons 2NH_3$$

The forward reaction is exothermic.

a   State **one** use of ammonia.   [1]

b   What is the meaning of the symbol $\rightleftharpoons$?   [1]

c   What are the sources of nitrogen and hydrogen used in the Haber process?   [2]

d   Name the catalyst in the Haber process.   [1]

e   i   If a temperature higher than 450 °C was used in the Haber process, what would happen to the **rate** of the reaction? Give a reason for your answer.   [2]

    ii If a temperature higher than 450 °C was used in the Haber process, what would happen to the **yield** of ammonia? Give a reason for your answer.   [2]

f   i   If a pressure higher than 200 atmospheres was used in the Haber process, what would happen to the **yield** of ammonia? Give a reason for your answer.   [2]

    ii Explain why the rate of reaction would be faster if the pressure was greater than 200 atmospheres.   [1]

    iii Suggest **one** reason why a pressure higher than 200 atmospheres is not used in the Haber process.   [1]

[Total: 13]

Cambridge IGCSE Chemistry (0620) Paper 32, Q3a–f March 2015

Here is a similar question on the Haber process. Attempt the question before reading the commentary. How different were your answers to the example student answers? Are there any areas where you feel you need to improve your understanding?

7 Ammonia is manufactured by the Haber process.

a The equation for the reaction is shown.

$$N_2(g) + 3H_2(g) \rightleftharpoons 2NH_3(g)$$

i State what is meant by the symbol $\rightleftharpoons$. [1]

ii State **one** source of hydrogen used in the manufacture of ammonia. [1]

b The table shows some data for the production of ammonia.

pressure /atm	temperature/°C	percentage yield of ammonia
250	350	58
100	450	28
400	450	42
250	550	20

Deduce the effect on the percentage yield of ammonia of:

- increasing the pressure of the reaction

- increasing the temperature of the reaction. [2]

c Explain, in terms of particles, what happens to the rate of this reaction when the temperature is increased. [3]

d Ammonia, NH_3, is used to produce nitric acid, HNO_3.
This happens in a three-stage process. **Stage 1** is a redox reaction.

$$4NH_3 + 5O_2 \rightarrow 4NO + 6H_2O$$

i Identify what is oxidised in **stage 1**. Give a reason for your answer. [2]

ii In this reaction the predicted yield of NO is 512 g. The actual yield is 384 g. Calculate the percentage yield of NO in this reaction. [1]

iii The equation for the reaction in **stage 2** is shown.

$$2NO + O_2 \rightarrow 2NO_2$$

Which major environmental problem does NO_2 cause if it is released into the atmosphere? [1]

iv The equation for the reaction in **stage 3** is shown. [4]

$$4NO_2 + 2H_2O + O_2 \rightarrow 4HNO_3$$

Calculate the volume of O_2 gas, at room temperature and pressure (r.t.p.), needed to produce 1260 g of HNO_3. Use the following steps.

Calculate the number of moles of HNO_3.

Deduce the number of moles of O_2 that reacted.

Calculate the volume of O_2 gas that reacts at room temperature and pressure (r.t.p.).

e   The reaction in **stage 3** is exothermic.

$$4NO_2 + 2H_2O + O_2 \rightarrow 4HNO_3$$

Complete the energy level diagram for this reaction. Include an arrow
that clearly shows the energy change during the reaction.   [3]

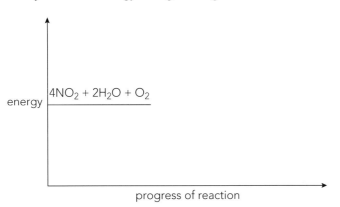

energy | $4NO_2 + 2H_2O + O_2$

progress of reaction

[Total: 18]

Cambridge IGCSE Chemistry (0620) Paper 43, Q2 June 2020

Example student response	Commentary
7 a i reversible	The student has demonstrated a good knowledge recall of the symbol and understands that this means a reversible reaction. *This answer is awarded 1 out of 1 mark.*
ii hydrogen gas	The input or reactant, which is hydrogen gas, has been indicated in the question. The question is asking for the source of this hydrogen gas. The student has not provided a source. *This answer is awarded 0 out of 1 mark.*
b decreases decreases	The student demonstrates good skills in being able to analyse the data in the table and recognise the pattern when increasing the temperature and the effect on the yield. Thus, one mark is awarded. A mistake has been made on the pressure as the values of the pressure are not arranged in increasing order. *This answer is awarded 1 out of 2 marks.*
c When the temperature increases, the rate of reaction increases.	The response showed that the student knows that temperature increases the rate of reaction. However, the response misses out the important point of what the question is asking in terms of particles. Hence, the response given has to be further developed in terms of the movement or collision of the particles, energy of the particles, etc. *This answer is awarded 0 out of 3 marks.*

Example student response	Commentary
d **i** NH_3 because reacts with $5O_2$	The student demonstrates a basic understanding that oxidation usually involves the reaction with oxygen and is able to identify NH_3 as the compound that has been oxidised. However, the explanation given uses the term 'reacts with $5O_2$' is simply restating the symbol equation given, instead of applying the knowledge of oxidation to show the gaining of oxygen that can be seen in the element's change in oxidation state or number. *This answer is awarded 1 out of 2 marks.*
ii 384/512 = 0.75	The response demonstrates a basic skill of calculating yield by dividing actual yield over predicted/theoretical yield. However, a slight mistake is made here where the student did not multiply by 100 for percentage. *This answer is awarded 0 out of 1 mark.*
iii causes acid rain	The student was able to recall how NO_2 can cause acid rain when released to the environment. *This answer is awarded 1 out of 1 mark.*

iv   moles of HNO_3
 	
     = 1260 g/(1 + 14 + 48)
 	
     = 1260 g/63
 	
     = 20
 	
moles of O_2
 	
     = 1260 g/(16 + 16)
 	
     = 1260 g/32
 	
     = 40
 	
volume of O_2
 	
40 x 24
 	
= 960 dm^3
	The student first demonstrated a good basic skill in calculating moles by applying the formula of dividing the mass with the molecular mass to obtain the moles of HNO_3. Thus, two marks are awarded here for showing the molecular mass and calculation of moles.
	
	However, a common error occurs when the question asks to determine the moles of another compound in the equation. Students should apply the ratio method of 1 O_2 : 4 HNO_3 and determine the moles of O_2 using the ratio. Hence, no marks are awarded here.
	
	This answer is awarded 2 out of 4 marks.

Example student response	Commentary
e 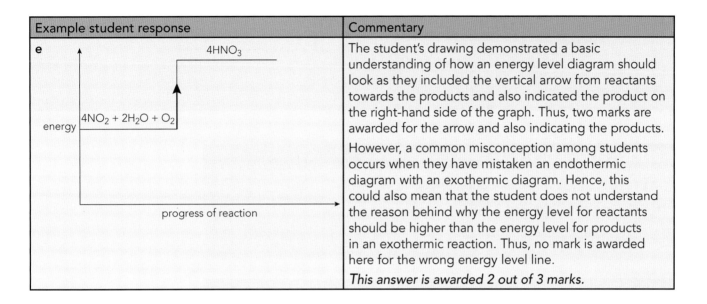	The student's drawing demonstrated a basic understanding of how an energy level diagram should look as they included the vertical arrow from reactants towards the products and also indicated the product on the right-hand side of the graph. Thus, two marks are awarded for the arrow and also indicating the products. However, a common misconception among students occurs when they have mistaken an endothermic diagram with an exothermic diagram. Hence, this could also mean that the student does not understand the reason behind why the energy level for reactants should be higher than the energy level for products in an exothermic reaction. Thus, no mark is awarded here for the wrong energy level line. *This answer is awarded 2 out of 3 marks.*

8   Now write an improved answer to the parts of Question 7 where you lost marks.
Use the commentary, and your knowledge from answering the previous questions,
to support you.

11 Acids and bases

KNOWLEDGE FOCUS

In this chapter you will answer questions on:

- the nature of acids and bases
- characteristic reactions of acids.

EXAM SKILLS FOCUS

In this chapter you will:

- show that you understand the 'identify' command word and answer 'identify' questions.

In this chapter you will answer a question that uses the command word 'identify'. 'Identify' questions often, but not always, ask you to choose from a list. It is important that you understand what this command word is instructing you to do:

Identify	name/select/recognise.

'Identify' questions may also ask you to name or recognise information from a diagram or trends from a graph. You might be asked to draw a label line or a cross on a diagram. Answers to 'identify' questions are often short responses, similar to the answers for 'state' or 'give' questions. When you answer the 'identify' question in this chapter, be clear in your response and try to spell key terms correctly.

11.1 The nature of acids and bases

1 Metal and non-metal oxides can be classified into acidic, basic, neutral or amphoteric. Create a table to identify the following oxides as acidic, basic, neutral or amphoteric.

| NO | NaOH | NO_2 | CO_2 | MgO | H_2O | Al_2O_3 |

2 Copy the text below and fill in the blanks using the words in the box.

| alkaline | hydroxide | equal | yellow |
| hydrogen | acidic | methyl orange | |

Hydrogen ions (H^+) and hydroxide ions (OH^-) are present in ....

concentrations in pure water. In an aqueous acidic solution there is a

higher concentration of .... ions compared to

.... ions. The indicator solutions litmus and

.... turn red in .... solutions. In an

.... solution, litmus turns blue and methyl orange turns

....

3 Identify the type of chemical reaction that occurs when hydrochloric acid reacts with sodium hydroxide.

Choose the correct answer from the words shown in the box.   **[Total: 1]**

| titration | neutralisation | electrolysis | fermentation |

UNDERSTAND THESE TERMS

- acid
- alkalis
- base
- corrosive
- indicator
- litmus
- methyl orange
- pH scale
- thymolphthalein
- universal indicator

≪ RECALL AND CONNECT 1 ≪

Copper(II) oxide, CuO, is a metal oxide that is formed when copper metal is heated with oxygen. What is the term used for the reaction where oxygen is gained?

11.2 Characteristic reactions of acids

1 Salts can be formed by the reactions of acids with metals, metal oxides, metal hydroxides, metal carbonates or metal hydrogen carbonates.

Write **two** word equations to show **two** different reactions between nitric acid and a suitable reactant to form the salt magnesium nitrate.

2 Some acids are stronger than others as they undergo a greater amount of dissociation when added to water.

   a State whether ethanoic acid or sulfuric acid is a strong acid. [1]

   b Describe **one** way to show that the acid you identified in **a** is a strong acid. [2]

   [Total: 3]

3 Nitric acid, HNO_3, is a strong acid.

   a State whether nitric acid dissociates completely or partially into ions when dissolved in water. [1]

   b Write a balanced symbol equation for the complete dissociation of sulfuric acid in water, including state symbols. [2]

   [Total: 3]

« RECALL AND CONNECT 2 «

During a metal displacement reaction, zinc atoms become Zn^{2+} ions, whereas Cu^{2+} ions become copper atoms. Which metal is the reducing agent in this reaction?

UNDERSTAND THESE TERMS

- dissociation
- strong acid
- weak acid

REFLECTION

How did you feel answering the questions in this chapter? Are there any areas that you could improve on?

Think about what you can do to improve on those areas. For example, make a mind map of the characteristics of acids and bases.

How can you monitor your progress in learning? For example, did you have enough practice writing word equations to represent the different reactions between acids and metals/metal compounds? Speak to your teacher if you are confused about the different products formed from different reactions of acids and see if there are more questions to practise with.

SELF-ASSESSMENT CHECKLIST

Let's revisit the Knowledge focus and Exam skills focus for this chapter.

Decide how confident you are with each statement.

Now I can:	Show it	Needs more work	Almost there	Confident to move on
describe acids and alkalis in terms of their effect on indicators	Compare the different characteristics of acids and alkalis and the colour changes that occur in indicators (litmus, methyl orange, thymolphthalein) when added to acids and alkalis.			
describe how bases are the oxides and hydroxides of metals; those bases that are soluble are referred to as alkalis	List the different types of bases and identify the bases that are soluble.			
describe how aqueous solutions of acids contain an excess of hydrogen ions, while alkaline solutions contain an excess of hydroxide ions	Describe acidic solutions and alkaline solutions in terms of hydrogen ions and hydroxide ions.			
compare the relative acidity or alkalinity, hydrogen ion concentration or pH of a solution using universal indicator	Distinguish between weak and strong acids by adding universal indicator and comparing the colour observed to the pH chart.			
describe how acids and alkalis react together in neutralisation reactions, and that bases displace ammonia from ammonium salts	Write word equations for the neutralisation reactions between acids and alkalis.			
describe how all metal oxides and hydroxides can act as bases, while many oxides of non-metals can be classified as acidic oxides	Categorise different examples of metal and non-metal oxides as basic oxides and acidic oxides.			
describe the characteristic reactions of acids	List the different types of reactions of acids.			

CONTINUED

Now I can:	Show it	Needs more work	Almost there	Confident to move on
describe how some metal oxides (amphoteric oxides) can react with both acids and alkalis	Write the word equation for the reaction between zinc oxide and hydrochloric acid and the word equation for the reaction between zinc oxide and sodium hydroxide.			
define strong and weak acids in terms of ion dissociation	Explain what the terms strong acid and weak acid mean.			
define an acid as a proton donor and a base as a proton acceptor	Distinguish between acids and bases in terms of proton transfer.			
show that I can understand the 'identify' command word and answer 'identify' questions.	Create a set of flashcards with the command words on one side, and their descriptions on the other.			

12 Preparation of salts

KNOWLEDGE FOCUS

In this chapter you will answer questions on:

- the importance of salts
- preparation of salts.

EXAM SKILLS FOCUS

In this chapter you will:

- show that you understand what a good response or answer looks like.

An important part of providing an appropriate response is knowing what a good response looks like. As you work through the Exam skill questions in this chapter, check your answers carefully against the answers provided and make a note of how these model answers are structured and where your answers differ. The Exam practice sections throughout this resource contain example student answers to real past paper questions with commentary and will help you to understand what a good response looks like.

12.1 The importance of salts

1 Copy and complete the Venn diagram in Figure 12.1 using the given labels to indicate whether each type of salt is soluble, insoluble or both.

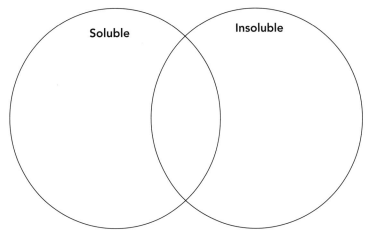

| sodium salts | carbonates | chlorides |
| ammonium salts | nitrates | sulfates |

Figure 12.1: Venn diagram

2 Match the hydrated salt to its correct colour.

| green | white | pink | blue |

| calcium sulfate | copper(II) sulfate | iron(II) sulfate | cobalt(II) chloride |

3 Define the term *water of crystallisation* and give **one** example. **[Total: 2]**

⟪ RECALL AND CONNECT 1 ⟫

Acids can react with metals, metal oxides, metal hydroxides or metal carbonates. All of these reactions produce a metal compound known as a metal salt. What is the name of the metal salt produced from the reaction between potassium hydroxide and nitric acid?

UNDERSTAND THESE TERMS

- anhydrous
- hydrated substance
- insoluble
- salts
- soluble
- water of crystallisation

12.2 Preparation of salts

1 The table shows three different methods used to prepare metal salts. Copy and complete this table by writing in the missing steps for each method.

Method 1	Method 2	Method 3
1 Add excess metal or solid to acid.	**1** Fill the burette with acid and flask with alkali.	**1** Add a soluble solution to another soluble solution.
2	**2**	**2**
3 Heat the filtrate to evaporate excess water and concentrate salt solution.	**3** Add acid into the flask and a few drops at a time until the indicator changes colour.	**3** Wash the solid with distilled water and dry in a warm oven.
4	**4** Repeat the experiment using the same known volume without using indicator to obtain the salt solution.	
5 Wash the crystals with a little distilled water and dry using filter paper.	**5**	
	6 Stop heating the solution and allow the solution to cool down for the crystals to form.	
	7	

2 A student added magnesium carbonate to dilute sulfuric acid. The reaction between the magnesium carbonate and dilute sulfuric acid produced a gas, water and a salt.

   a Identify the gas and salt formed in this reaction. [1]

   b In a second experiment, the student reacted magnesium metal and dilute hydrochloric acid to produce a different magnesium salt.

   Explain why the student could use sodium carbonate but not sodium metal to obtain a sodium salt. [2]

   [Total: 3]

3 The reaction between aqueous lead(II) nitrate and aqueous sodium sulfate produces an insoluble salt.

   a Give the name of the insoluble salt formed. [1]

   b State the term used for this type of reaction. [1]

   [Total: 2]

> **UNDERSTAND THESE TERMS**
> - burette
> - end-point
> - ionic equation
> - precipitation
> - titration
> - volumetric pipette

≪ RECALL AND CONNECT 2 ≪

In the titration method, neutralisation of an acid by an alkali takes place to form a soluble salt. An indicator is added to determine the end-point of titration (or neutralisation point). Methyl orange is a common indicator used. What colour would methyl orange turn if added to an alkaline solution?

REFLECTION

Were you able to answer all the questions correctly in this chapter? Did you find that comparing your answers to the ones provided helped you understand what a good response looks like?

Try writing down three examples of soluble salts and three examples of insoluble salts. How will you check if you have improved your understanding? For example, are you able to write down the steps used to prepare a sample of pure, dry magnesium sulfate? Review and test yourself regularly on the topic in this chapter and check your progress with the self-assessment checklist.

SELF-ASSESSMENT CHECKLIST

Let's revisit the Knowledge focus and Exam skills focus for this chapter.

Decide how confident you are with each statement.

Now I can:	Show it	Needs more work	Almost there	Confident to move on
understand that salts are an important group of ionic compounds	List uses for a few examples of salt compounds.			
describe how some salts are soluble in water, while others are insoluble	Create a table to categorise examples of soluble and insoluble salts.			
describe the general solubility rules for various different types of salt	List some features that can be used to determine whether the salt is soluble or insoluble.			
define hydrated and anhydrous substances in terms of water content	Write out the meaning of the terms hydrated and anhydrous.			
describe the preparation, separation and purification of soluble salts by reaction of the parent acid with either excess metal, excess insoluble base or excess insoluble carbonate	Write out the methods used to prepare soluble salts and insoluble salts.			

CONTINUED

Now I can:	Show it	Needs more work	Almost there	Confident to move on
describe the preparation, separation and purification of a soluble salt by titration of an acid with an alkali	List the apparatus, name of an indicator and steps required to prepare a soluble salt using the titration method.			
define the term water of crystallisation	Write out the meaning of the term water of crystallisation.			
describe the preparation and separation of insoluble salts by precipitation	List the examples of solutions and steps used to prepare an insoluble salt, e.g. barium sulfate.			
show that I understand what a good response or answer looks like.	Attempt Question 2 in Exam practice 4 and compare your answers to the sample answers and commentary.			

13 The Periodic Table

Questions may ask you to analyse given information and write down a conclusion with evidence that can be found in the given information or Periodic Table. These types of questions may have a command word such as 'state' or 'identify', and then ask you to 'justify' your answer. You need to explain how you reached your answer using the evidence or given information.

13.1 Classifying the elements

1 Copy the table and write down the correct term to describe the elements organised in the Periodic Table in the column on the right for each description.

Descriptions	Terms
Elements found in Groups I to VIII of the Periodic Table.	
Elements that are metals and found in the central region of the Periodic Table, between Groups II and III.	
The group in which the element lithium (Li) is found.	
Elements that are unreactive gases.	

2 Figure 13.1 shows an outline of the Periodic Table.

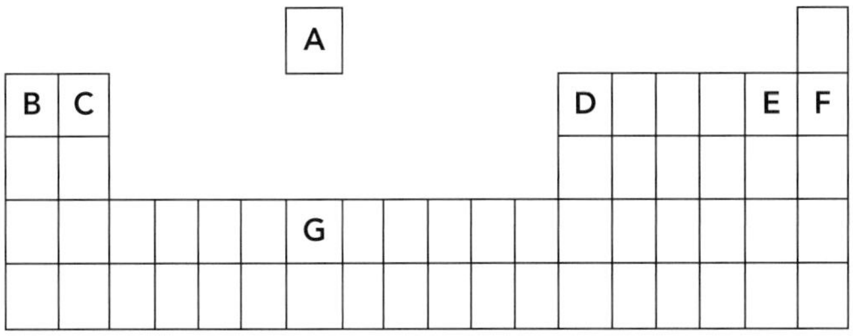

Figure 13.1: Outline of the Periodic Table

Copy the table and use the information shown in the Periodic Table in Figure 13.1 to complete it by writing the letters of the elements matching each category. Each letter can only be used once.

Metals	Metalloids (semi-metals)	Non-metals	Gases

3 A beryllium atom has an atomic number of 4 and a magnesium atom has an atomic number of 12.

From these two elements, identify the one in which the group number and period number are the same. Justify your answer. **[Total: 2]**

≪ RECALL AND CONNECT 1 ≪

Halogens are able to produce a series of compounds with other elements as ions, such as chlorides, bromides and iodides. One example is chloride salts. Which **two** chloride salts are insoluble in water?

UNDERSTAND THESE TERMS

- alkali metals
- groups
- noble gas
- Periodic Table
- periods
- transition elements

REFLECTION

Look back at your answer to Exam skill Question 3 in this section – did you remember to give reasons or an explanation for the element you identified in order to score the second mark?

13.2 Trends in groups

1 Copy and complete the following table about the Group VII elements by placing the correct descriptions into the correct categories.

pale-green grey red-brown solid liquid gas
relative atomic mass of 127 relative atomic mass of 35.5
relative atomic mass of 80

Chlorine	Bromine	Iodine

2 Table 13.1 shows the properties of some Group II elements.

Element	Atomic radius ($\times 10^{-12}$ m)	Melting point in °C
beryllium	99	1287
magnesium	140	650
calcium		842
strontium	190	

Table 13.1

a Examine the data in Table 13.1 and state a trend in the physical properties of Group II elements. [1]

b Predict the atomic radius of calcium. [1]

c Explain why it is difficult to predict the melting point of strontium. [1]

[Total: 3]

3 Table 13.2 shows the properties of some Group I elements.

Element	Reaction with water
lithium	fizzes slowly forming bubbles
sodium	fizzes rapidly forming many bubbles
potassium	fizzes very rapidly forming very many bubbles

Table 13.2

a Describe the trend in the reactivity of the elements as you go down Group I. [1]

b Identify the gas formed when Group I elements react with water. [1]

c A few drops of universal indicator are added to the water solution after adding Group I elements. Explain why the solution turned purple. [1]

[Total: 3]

> **UNDERSTAND THESE TERMS**
> - halides
> - halogens
> - halogen displacement reactions

13.3 Trends across a period

1 Copy and complete the sentences. Use the words provided to fill in the blanks of this paragraph that describes the trends across a period in the Periodic Table. Each word is only used once.

non-metallic	across	decrease	period
acidic	basic	down	increase

As you move .... any group in the Periodic Table there is a trend in the chemical properties.

As you move .... a period in the Periodic Table, there is a trend in physical properties. For example, moving across from Group I to Group IV the melting points and boiling points of the elements .... and moving across to Group VIII they ....

The elements in Groups I to III of Period 2 are metallic elements. The elements in Groups IV to VIII are ....

There is also a trend in the chemical properties. As you move across a .... in the Periodic Table, the oxides of the elements change from being .... oxides to being .... oxides.

2 Tungsten is a transition element.

a State **one** property of tungsten that is different to properties of elements in Group I. [1]

b State **one** other property of a transition element that is different from those elements in Group II of the Periodic Table. [1]

[Total: 2]

3 Chromium has high melting point and high corrosion resistance.

  a Give the name for the elements in the part of the Periodic Table that chromium is found in. [1]

  b Describe **one** property of chromium that is similar to the property of a Group I element. [1]

  [Total: 2]

UNDERSTAND THIS TERM

- oxidation number

≪ RECALL AND CONNECT 2 ≪

Copper can form compounds containing copper(I) ions (Cu^+) and copper(II) ions (Cu^{2+}). What is the colour of a copper(II) sulfate hydrated salt?

REFLECTION

Are there any areas that you think you did well in? What are the areas you think you could improve on? Write them down.

Now write down what you will do to strengthen your learning for these areas. For example, identify the group number and period number for a specific element using their electronic structure.

How can you check that you understand the concepts in this chapter? For example, are you able to describe two trends down a group and two trends across a period of the Periodic Table? Don't forget to keep recalling and practising the key terms needed for this chapter. If you are still unclear about the properties of transition metals then speak to your teacher.

SELF-ASSESSMENT CHECKLIST

Let's revisit the Knowledge focus and Exam skills focus for this chapter.

Decide how confident you are with each statement.

Now I can:	Show it	Needs more work	Almost there	Confident to move on
describe how the elements are organised into a table of periods and groups based on the order of increasing atomic (proton) number	Write down how elements are organised in the Periodic Table and then compare your answer to the Periodic Table.			
describe the relationship between the group number and ionic charge of the elements	Compare the group numbers and ionic charges of specific elements (e.g. Na^+, Mg^{2+}, Al^{3+}).			
explain the similarities in chemical properties of the elements in a group	List the similarities in the chemical properties of the elements in a group.			

CONTINUED

Now I can:	Show it	Needs more work	Almost there	Confident to move on
describe the trends in properties of the Group I alkali metals	Draw an outline of the Periodic Table and add labelled arrows on the side of the outline to indicate the trends in properties down Group I.			
describe the trends in properties of the halogens (Group VII)	Draw an outline of the Periodic Table and add labelled arrows on the side of the outline to indicate the trends in properties down Group VII.			
describe the noble gases (Group VIII) as unreactive, monatomic gases	Write down the typical characteristics of the Group VIII elements.			
describe the change from metallic to non-metallic character across a period	Draw an outline of the Periodic Table and add labelled arrows on the side of the outline to indicate the trends in properties across Period 2 or 3.			
describe the key characteristics of the transition elements	Write down three characteristics of the transition elements.			
identify trends in groups given information on the elements	List the trends down a group and across a period.			
describe the ability of the transition elements to form ions with variable oxidation numbers	Write down the characteristics of transition elements and the reason they can form different oxide compounds.			
understand how to justify an answer.	Write a an exam-style question and mark scheme that requires you to give an answer and then justify it.			

Exam practice 4

This section contains past paper questions from previous Cambridge exams, which draw together your knowledge on a range of topics that you have covered up to this point. These questions give you the opportunity to test your knowledge and understanding. Additional past paper practice questions can be found in the accompanying digital material.

The following question has an example student response and commentary provided. Once you have worked through the question, read the student response and commentary. Are your answers different to the sample answers?

1   a   The structures of five organic compounds, **A**, **B**, **C**, **D** and **E**, are shown. Answer the questions that follow. Each letter may be used once, more than once or not at all.

i   Give the letter of the compound that is propan-1-ol. [1]

ii   Give the letter of the compound that has the empirical formula CH_2. [1]

iii Give the letter of **one** compound that reacts with bromine in an addition reaction. [1]

iv   Give the letter of **one** compound that reacts with chlorine to form the compound shown. [1]

v   Give the letters of **two** compounds that can react with each other to form an ester. [1]

vi   Give the letter of the compound that is in the same homologous series as hex-1-ene. [1]

vii Give the letter of **one** compound that is an acid. [1]

viii Draw a structural isomer of compound D.
Show all of the atoms and all of the bonds. [1]

b Some acids are described as weak acids. State the meaning of the term
weak acid. [2]

weak:

acid:

[Total: 10]

Cambridge IGCSE Chemistry (0620) Paper 43, Q1 June 2020

Example student response	Commentary
1 a i D	The student identified the propanol compound correctly. This shows good skills in applying organic chemistry concepts to identify the correct functional group and correct number of carbon atoms for propanol. *This answer is awarded 1 out of 1 mark.*
ii C	The correct response here again showed good application skills in understanding the concept of empirical formula and being able to determine the empirical from the structural formula of given compounds. *This answer is awarded 1 out of 1 mark.*
iii B	The student's response here identified an incorrect compound that reacts with bromine in an addition reaction. This might be a common misconception among students. Alkanes can also react with bromine, however, it is not known as an addition reaction but a substitution reaction. *This answer is awarded 0 out of 1 mark.*
iv B	The student identified the compound correctly based on a similar structural formula diagram given. This demonstrated good knowledge recall of how alkane is able to react with chlorine to form a chloroalkane. *This answer is awarded 1 out of 1 mark.*
v D, E	The student demonstrated good knowledge recall of how esters are formed from carboxylic acid and alcohol. The student identified both the compounds correctly. *This answer is awarded 1 out of 1 mark.*
vi C	The student demonstrated good application skills in being able to identify another alkene correctly. *This answer is awarded 1 out of 1 mark.*
vii E	Here, the student identified the carboxylic acid correctly as they had also been able to answer Question (v) correctly by identifying the component that forms an ester. *This answer is awarded 1 out of 1 mark.*
viii a drawing of a correct isomer for propan-1-ol	The student demonstrated good knowledge of organic chemistry in which a correct isomer is shown. *This answer is awarded 1 out of 1 mark.*

Example student response	Commentary
b weak – partially ionize to form ions acid – lose protons or hydrogen ions	This question helps students in tackling the question better as the terms 'weak' and 'acid' have been listed separately to give the idea to the student that they have to define both terms correctly. Usually, some students might not define acid but just the term 'weak' when given the term 'weak acid' together. *This answer is awarded 2 out of 2 marks.*

Now write an improved answer to the parts of Question 1 where you did not score highly. You will need to carefully work back through each part of the question, ensuring that you include enough detail and clearly explain each point. Use the commentary to guide you as you answer.

The following question has an example student response and commentary provided.

Once you have worked through the question, compare your answer to the student response and commentary.

2　**a**　Brass is an alloy of copper and zinc.

　　i　Which **one** of the following diagrams best represents an alloy?　　[1]

J 　K 　L 　M

　　ii　Brass is used to make the propellers of ships rather than pure copper or pure zinc. Suggest a property of brass which explains this.　　[1]

　b　The chemical equation for the reaction of zinc with concentrated nitric acid is shown.

$$Zn + 4HNO_3 \rightarrow Zn(NO_3)_2 + 2NO_2 + 2H_2O$$

　　i　Complete the word equation for this reaction.　　[2]

zinc	+	nitric acid	→		+		+	

　　ii　One of the compounds in this equation is a pollutant gas which contributes to acid rain. Identify the pollutant gas and state a common source of it.

　　pollutant gas:

　　source:　　[2]

　c　Zinc oxide is reduced by heating it with carbon.

$$ZnO + C \rightarrow Zn + CO$$

　　How does this equation show that zinc oxide is reduced?　　[1]

d When green iron(II) sulfate is heated it loses its water of crystallisation. The reaction is reversible.

   i Complete the following equation by writing the sign for a reversible reaction. [1]

$$FeSO_4.7H_2O \qquad FeSO_4 + 7H_2O$$
   green $\quad$ .... $\quad$ white

   ii Use the information in the equation to suggest how to change white iron(II) sulfate into green iron(II) sulfate. [1]

[Total: 9]

Cambridge IGCSE Chemistry (0620) Paper 33, Q3 November 2018

Example student response	Commentary
2 a i L	The student was able to identify alloys correctly based on the diagram and could distinguish between the arrangement of particles in pure metals and alloys. *This answer is awarded 1 out of 1 mark.*
ii can withstand corrosion	The student's response showed a good knowledge recall of the properties of alloys compared to pure metals and their applications. *This answer is awarded 1 out of 1 mark.*
b i zinc + nitric acid → zinc nitrogen oxide + nitrogen oxide + water	The response here demonstrated a slight lack of skills in understanding chemical formulae. The student was unable to identify the correct chemicals from the formulae provided. *This answer is awarded 0 out of 2 marks.*
ii pollutant gas – NO_2 source – lightning	The response showed that the student was able to identify the pollutant gas even though they gave the formula rather than the name. One mark is still awarded for being able to identify the pollutant gas. The student was also able to identify the source of the pollutant gas correctly, hence another mark is awarded here. *This answer is awarded 2 out of 2 marks.*
c zinc oxide loses oxygen	The response here showed a good understanding of the redox reaction and that the student was able to apply that understanding based on the equation given. *This answer is awarded 1 out of 1 mark.*
d i ⇌	The student showed a good knowledge recall of the reversible reaction arrow symbol correctly. *This answer is awarded 1 out of 1 mark.*
ii addition of water	The student demonstrated a good understanding of the term 'water of crystallisation' and was able to apply the understanding based on the equation. *This answer is awarded 1 out of 1 mark.*

Now try another similar question. Use the previous commentaries to support you as you answer.

3   **a**   A list of formulae is shown below.

$AlCl_3$	CO_2	$MgCl_2$	NH_3
$CaCO_3$	$CoCl_2$	N_2	O_2
CO	$CuSO_4$	$NaCl$	SO_2

Answer the following questions using these formulae. Each formula may be used once, more than once or not at all. State which formula represents:

i   a compound that changes colour from white to blue when water is added   [1]

ii   an element that forms 78% of clean, dry air   [1]

iii   a compound that contains an ion with a single positive charge   [1]

iv   a compound that dissolves in water to form an alkaline solution.   [1]

b   Complete the dot-and-cross diagram to show the electron arrangement in a molecule of ammonia.   [2]

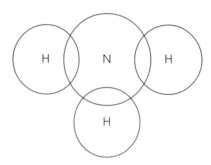

c   State whether magnesium oxide is a basic oxide or an acidic oxide. Give a reason for your answer.   [1]

[Total: 7]

Cambridge IGCSE Chemistry (0620) Paper 31, Q1 November 2021

The following question has an example student response and commentary provided. Once you have worked through the question, compare your answer to the student response and commentary. Were your answers different to the example responses? In which ways were they different?

4   This question is about Group I and Group VII elements.

a   Deduce the number of electrons, neutrons and protons in one atom of the isotope of potassium shown.   [3]

$$^{40}_{19}K$$

number of electrons:

number of neutrons:

number of protons:

b Complete the chemical equation for the reaction of potassium with water
   to form potassium hydroxide and a gas which pops with a lighted splint. [2]

$$2K + ...H_2O \rightarrow 2KOH + ...$$

c The table shows some properties of four Group I elements.

element	melting point/°C	boiling point/°C	relative hardness
lithium	181	1342	5.0
sodium	....	883	0.7
potassium	63	760	....
rubidium	39	686	0.2

   i Complete the table by predicting:

   - the melting point of sodium

   - the relative hardness of potassium. [2]

   ii Predict the physical state of potassium at 100 °C.
   Give a reason for your answer. [2]

d Aqueous bromine reacts with aqueous potassium iodide.

$$Br_2 + 2KI \rightarrow 2KBr + I_2$$

   i Explain how this equation shows that bromine is more reactive
   than iodine. [2]

   ii State the colour of aqueous iodine. [1]

e Bromine is a diatomic molecule. State the meaning of the term *diatomic*. [1]

f Bromine liquid turns into a gas very easily at room temperature.
   Choose the word which best describes a substance that evaporates easily.
   Draw a circle around your chosen answer.

   conductor　　　**flammable**　　　**malleable**　　　**volatile** [1]

   [Total: 14]

Cambridge IGCSE Chemistry (0620) Paper 32, Q3 June 2022

Example student response	Commentary
4 a 21 19 19	A mistake commonly made by students is confusing the number of neutrons for the number of electrons. Even though neutrons are found in the nucleus with protons, their numbers are not the same. The number of neutrons is calculated by subtracting the atomic number, 19, from the mass number, 40. The number of electrons is the same as the number of protons for a neutral atom. ***This answer is awarded 1 out of 3 marks.***
b $2H_2O$ H_2	The student's response showed a good recall of the products formed in a reaction between metals and water as well as being able to balance the equation. One mark is awarded for the correct product and another mark is awarded for the correct number used to balance the equation. ***This answer is awarded 2 out of 2 marks.***

Example student response	Commentary
c **i** melting point – 174 hardness – 0.5	The student demonstrated a good ability to analyse the data from a table. By observing the pattern given, the student was able to produce a written answer that falls within the accepted range. ***This answer is awarded 2 out of 2 marks.***
ii gas boiling point of water is at 100°C	The response here showed that the student was not able to discern the state of matter using the given information of melting point and boiling point. This question requires skills in application and making connections between the concepts of states of matter and the melting point and boiling point. No mark is awarded for the incorrect state of matter. Hence, the explanation given also shows the lack of knowledge and skill in making connections between concepts. No mark is awarded here. ***This answer is awarded 0 out of 2 marks.***
d **i** Bromine is located above iodine in the Periodic Table. The reactivity is decreasing down the group.	The response showed a lack of skill in making connections between the concepts of halogen reactivity and the equation given. The student was not able to discern the reactivity from the equation and also did not read the question, which asked them to 'explain how this equation shows'. This means the answer should be based on the equation. The student needs to be able to write about the displacement reaction happening in the equation. ***This answer is awarded 0 out of 2 marks.***
ii brown	The student demonstrated a good knowledge recall of the halogen colours. ***This answer is awarded 1 out of 1 mark.***
e molecule has two atoms	The response here again showed a good recall of the definition of the term 'diatomic'. This student demonstrated good recall skills when it comes to direct questions that do not require a high level of application skills. ***This answer is awarded 1 out of 1 mark.***
f volatile	Similar to the responses seen in parts **(d)(ii)** and **(e)**, the student was able to answer questions that are direct questioning of a knowledge recall and do not require any application skills. Here, the student demonstrated a good recall of the term for substances that evaporate easily. ***This answer is awarded 1 out of 1 mark.***

Now try another similar question. Use the knowledge you have gained from answering the previous questions to support you.

5   This question is about elements in the Periodic Table.

The table shows some properties of five elements, **P**, **Q**, **R**, **S** and **T**.

element	melting point/°C	density in g/cm³	electrical conductivity of the solid	atomic radius/nm
P	1535	7.86	very good	0.125
Q	−7	3.12	does not conduct	0.114
R	1495	8.90	very good	0.126
S	−157	0.0035	does not conduct	0.110
T	839	1.54	very good	0.174

a   Use only the elements shown in the table to answer this question.

State which two of the elements, **P**, **Q**, **R**, **S** and **T**, are covalent molecules. Give **two** reasons for your answer.   [3]

b   Element **T** is on the left-hand side of the Periodic Table. Suggest whether its oxide is acidic or basic. Give a reason for your answer.   [1]

c   Krypton is an element in Group VIII of the Periodic Table. Explain, using ideas about electronic structure, why krypton is unreactive.   [1]

d   Sodium is an element in Group I of the Periodic Table. Iron is a transition element. Iron has a higher melting point and higher boiling point than sodium.

Give **two** other ways in which the properties of transition elements differ from the properties of Group I elements.   [2]

e   The table compares the reactivity of four metals with dilute hydrochloric acid.

metal	reaction with dilute hydrochloric acid
calcium	reacts very rapidly
copper	no reaction
iron	reacts rapidly
nickel	reacts slowly

Put the four metals in order of their reactivity. Put the least reactive metal first.   [2]

least reactive ⟶ most reactive

f   Hot iron reacts with steam. The reaction is reversible. Complete the equation by writing the symbol for a reversible reaction.   [1]

$$3Fe + 4H_2O \quad .... \quad Fe_3O_4 + 4H_2$$

g   Steel is an *alloy* of iron. State the meaning of the term alloy.   [1]

[Total: 11]

Cambridge IGCSE Chemistry (0620) Paper 31, Q8 June 2021

14 Metallic elements and alloys

In order to understand exam questions better, you need to know what command words are and what they mean. In this chapter you will answer questions with the command word 'give'. 'Give' questions require a short answer, usually a word(s) or a statement. When you attempt the 'give' questions in this chapter, think about whether you fully understand what this command word means and what is required in answers to questions containing this command word.

| Give | produce an answer from a given source or recall/memory. |

14.1 The properties of metals

1   Copy and complete the table by adding the physical properties of metals and non-metals listed in the box.

> sonorous   dull surface   good thermal conductors
> poor electrical conductor   brittle   high melting and boiling points

Metals	Non-metals

2   Physical properties can be used to differentiate metals from non-metals. For instance, the shape of a metal can be changed by hammering, whereas non-metals break easily when hit.

    a   Give the term used to describe the property of a metal that allows it to be beaten or bent into different shapes.   [1]

    b   Explain how the structure of metal allows it to easily change shape when a force is applied.   [2]

[Total: 3]

3   Magnesium metal can react with steam, oxygen and dilute hydrochloric acid.

    a   Give the word equation for the reaction between magnesium and steam.   [1]

    b   Give the symbol equation, including state symbols, for the reaction between magnesium and oxygen.   [2]

    c   Identify the salt and gas produced when magnesium reacts with dilute hydrochloric acid.   [1]

[Total: 4]

> **UNDERSTAND THESE TERMS**
> - ductility
> - electrical conductivity
> - malleability
> - sonorous
> - thermal conductivity

≪ RECALL AND CONNECT 1 ≪

Metals can be found on the left side of the Periodic Table, whereas non-metals can be found on the right side of the Periodic Table. What is the name given to the Group 7 elements in the Periodic Table?

14.2 Uses of metals

1   Copy and complete the sentences, using words from the list.

> ductile   metals   magnesium   electrical
> steel   iron   zinc   left

Most elements in the Periodic Table can be classified as .... These elements are positioned to the .... of the Periodic Table. Metals can be used for a variety of purposes due to their physical properties. For example, ... is used to make bridge structures and cooking pots and pans. Copper is often used in electrical cables and wiring because of its high .... conductivity and the fact that it is very .... is often used as a protective coating on iron and steel objects.

2   Copper is one of the least reactive metals.

   a   Give **one** physical property of copper.   [1]
   b   Explain why pure copper is used for circuit boards and wiring instead of alloys.   [1]

[Total: 2]

14.3 Alloys

1   Copy and complete the Venn diagram in Figure 14.1 to show **two** similarities and **two** differences between alloys and pure metals.

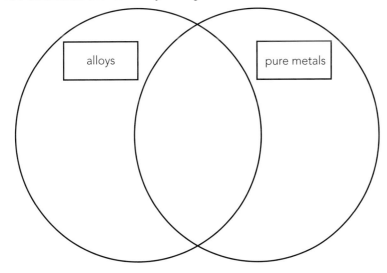

Figure 14.1: Venn diagram of alloys and pure metals

2 Bronze is an alloy that is made up of copper and tin elements.
Sketch the arrangement of atoms in bronze and label the elements. **[Total: 2]**

3 Chromium has a high melting point and makes up 18% of the alloy stainless steel.

    a Give **one** use of stainless steel. [1]

    b Explain how the structure of an alloy makes it stronger than pure metal. [2]

[Total: 3]

> UNDERSTAND THESE TERMS
> - alloys
> - brass
> - stainless steel

≪ RECALL AND CONNECT 2 ≪

Mild steel is an alloy that is made up of 99.7% iron and 0.3% carbon.
Iron is a transition metal. State one property of transition metals.

REFLECTION

Have you successfully memorised the definitions of the key terms in this chapter? How do you know? You could test yourself by making cards with the term on one side and the definition on the other. If you don't recall them all, then test yourself every few days until you can. By doing this, you can avoid trying to memorise a lot of information in a short space of time just before the exam which can cause anxiety and is not a good way to prepare. What other ways can you think of that will help you to remember and recall the knowledge that you need?

SELF-ASSESSMENT CHECKLIST

Let's revisit the Knowledge focus and Exam skills focus for this chapter.

Decide how confident you are with each statement.

Now I can:	Show it	Needs more work	Almost there	Confident to move on
understand the differences in the physical properties of metals and non-metals	Create a table to compare the physical properties of metals and non-metals.			
describe the reactions of metals with water, acids and oxygen	Write the word and balanced symbol equations for reactions of metals (e.g. magnesium, calcium) with water, acids and oxygen.			
explore and appreciate the usefulness of metallic elements	List a few examples of metals and their uses.			
describe how alloys are mixtures of metals with other elements	List a few examples of alloys and their compositions.			

CONTINUED

Now I can:	Show it	Needs more work	Almost there	Confident to move on
describe how diagrams can be used to represent the physical structure of alloys	Sketch the structure of an alloy showing the main atoms and added element.			
understand the uses of certain alloys in terms of their physical properties	List down a few types of alloys with their uses and physical properties that make them suitable for their uses.			
consider how alloys can be harder or stronger than pure metals	Write a paragraph explaining why alloys can be harder or stronger than the pure metal.			
understand the 'give' command word and answer 'give' questions.	Say what the command word 'give' means and why you think it was chosen as the command word for the questions in this chapter.			

15 Reactivity of metals

KNOWLEDGE FOCUS

In this chapter you will answer questions on:

- the metal reactivity series

 metal displacement reactions.

EXAM SKILLS FOCUS

In this chapter you will:

- show that you understand what the command word 'analyse' means when used in a question.

Sometimes, questions ask you to analyse something, before you explain or identify an answer.

| Analyse | examine in detail to show meaning, identify elements and the relationship between them. |

Analysing ionic half-equations is one of the questions which would involve understanding the differences between the half-equations and their connection to the redox reaction. There will be questions that require you to analyse displacement equations and to identify the most and/or least reactive metals.

15.1 The metal reactivity series

1   Copy and complete the table to show the order of reactivity of metals from most reactive to least reactive.

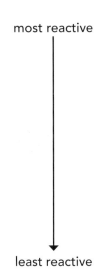

Metals
potassium
calcium
zinc
iron
copper
gold

most reactive

least reactive

2   The table shows the observations of different metals reacting with dilute hydrochloric acid. Arrange the metals in increasing order of reactivity.

Metal A	Metal B	Metal C	Metal D	Metal E
no reaction	rapid bubbling, metal dissolves quickly	slow bubbling, metal dissolves slowly	fast bubbling only upon heating, metal dissolves	bubbles around the metal

3   A student conducted two experiments to investigate displacement reactions of two different metals.

Experiment 1: Aluminium metal is added to a solution of zinc nitrate.

Experiment 2: Copper metal is added to a solution of zinc nitrate.

a   Predict whether a reaction will occur in each experiment.   [1]

Experiment 1: ....

Experiment 2: ....

b   Give a balanced symbol equation for any reaction that occurs in the experiments. Write 'no reaction' if none occurs.   [2]

Experiment 1: ....

Experiment 2: ....

[Total: 3]

≪ RECALL AND CONNECT 1 ≪

Aluminium is located above iron in the reactivity series. Which physical property of aluminium makes it suitable to be used in overhead power lines?

UNDERSTAND THESE TERMS

- reactivity
- reactivity series (of metals)

15.2 Metal displacement reactions

1 Figure 15.1 shows the displacement reaction of three different metals, P, Q and T.

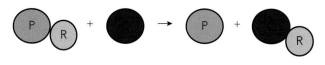

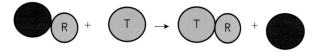

Figure 15.1

Arrange the metals in decreasing order of reactivity.

2 Chlorine is a pale yellow green gas. When chlorine reacts with aqueous sodium iodide, sodium chloride and iodine are formed. The reaction is represented by the symbol equation shown:

$$Cl_2 + 2NaI \rightarrow 2NaCl + I_2$$

Analyse the symbol equation above and explain how this equation shows that iodine is less reactive than chlorine. [1]

[Total: 1]

3 A student is investigating a displacement reaction by adding copper metal, Cu, to aqueous silver nitrate $AgNO_3$.

The ionic half-equations for the reaction are shown below.

a Copy and complete the ionic half-equations. [1]

1	$Cu(s) \rightarrow$ ....(aq) + 2e$^-$
2	$2Ag^+(aq) + 2e^- \rightarrow 2$..............(s)

b A displacement reaction is an example of a redox reaction.
Identify which of the two ionic half-equations represents the oxidation reaction. Explain your answer. [2]

[Total: 3]

≪ RECALL AND CONNECT 2 ≪

Magnesium is more reactive than copper and is able to react with dilute hydrochloric acid to form a salt and a gas. What is the name of the gas produced?

UNDERSTAND THIS TERM

- displacement reaction

REFLECTION

Did you find it difficult to answer the 'analyse' Exam skills question? Were you able to successfully examine the information provided and identify the meaning and relationship between elements?

Were there any concepts in the chapter you were unsure about? Identify these and then consider how you could practise them. For example, write down two metals that are more reactive than iron and write a word equation to show the reaction between both metals with dilute hydrochloric acid. How will you check that you have increased your understanding? Are you able to write down a balanced symbol equation for the reaction between lithium and water?

Speak to your teacher if you are confused about the redox reaction for the ionic half-equations.

SELF-ASSESSMENT CHECKLIST

Let's revisit the Knowledge focus and Exam skills focus for this chapter.

Decide how confident you are with each statement.

Now I can:	Show it	Needs more work	Almost there	Confident to move on
establish the concept of a reactivity series	List the metals in decreasing order of reactivity to show the reactivity series.			
analyse how different metals show differences in the strength of their reaction with water and dilute acid	Write word and balanced symbol equations to show the reaction of metals (e.g. magnesium, aluminium) with water and dilute acid.			
understand that some metals react very strongly with water or acid, while others do not react at all	Create a table that places different metals in order of their reactivities based on their reactions with water.			
describe how this reactivity relates to the reactivity series and predict an order of reactivity given a set of experimental results	Practise some exam-style questions to extract or analyse information given and arrange metals in increasing/decreasing order of reactivity.			

CONTINUED

Now I can:	Show it	Needs more work	Almost there	Confident to move on
analyse how the different levels of reactivity of metals can be used to organise them into a reactivity series	Create a reactivity series to show the metals arranged in order of increasing/ decreasing reactivity.			
understand that the reactivity series relates to the ease with which a metal forms its positive ion by considering the displacement reactions of metals	Write word equations to represent displacement reactions (e.g. magnesium and copper sulfate).			
understand that these displacement reactions are redox reactions	Write ionic half-equations of displacement reactions (e.g. copper and silver nitrate) and indicate which half-equation represents oxidation and which half-equation represents reduction.			
understand what the word 'analyse' means when used in a question.	Compare your answer to the question that contains the word 'analyse' with the answer provided and see if you understand what you had to do.			

16 Extraction and corrosion of metals

KNOWLEDGE FOCUS

In this chapter you will answer questions on:

- metal extraction and the reactivity series
- corrosion of metals.

EXAM SKILLS FOCUS

In this chapter you will:

- continue to think about your own learning and the revision strategies that work best for you.

As you work through the questions in this chapter think back to the different learning strategies that you have been introduced to throughout this book. Which strategies work best for your ways of learning?

Continue using the reflection features and self-assessment checklist at the end of the chapter to help you reflect on your learning.

Further support is available in the exam skills chapter at the start of this book.

16.1 Metal extraction and the reactivity series

1   Arrange the following processes to show the correct order of extraction of iron from iron ore. The first process has been numbered for you.

Processes	Order
Carbon dioxide reacts with more carbon and is reduced to carbon monoxide.	------
Limestone is added to remove impurities.	------
Carbon (coke) burns in the air, reacting with oxygen to produce carbon dioxide.	1
Limestone undergoes thermal decomposition to produce calcium oxide.	------
Iron(III) oxide is reduced by carbon monoxide to form iron and carbon dioxide.	------
Calcium oxide reacts with silica to form slag, which can then be removed separately.	------

2   Copy and complete the paragraph about the extraction of aluminium from its ore. Fill in the blanks using words from the box.

electrolysed	electrolysis	sodium hydroxide	bauxite	cryolite

.... is the major ore of aluminium, also known as aluminium oxide, Al_2O_3. Aluminium is extracted from the ore using .... The ore is first treated with .... to obtain pure aluminium oxide (alumina). The aluminium oxide is then dissolved in molten .... The molten mixture is then .... to obtain pure aluminium.

3   Iron ore contains iron(III) oxide.

   a   State the name of an iron ore.   [1]

   b   State the method used to extract iron from iron oxide.   [1]

                                                              [Total: 2]

UNDERSTAND THESE TERMS

- bauxite
- blast furnace
- corrosion
- cryolite
- electrolysis
- electrolyte
- electrolytic cell
- hematite
- limestone
- mineral
- ore
- slag

≪ RECALL AND CONNECT 1 ≪

Aluminium is extracted from its ore using electrolysis, whereas iron is extracted from its ore using reduction by carbon. Which metal is located at a higher position in the reactivity series?

16.2 Corrosion of metals

1   The following table shows descriptions of different methods of rust prevention.
    Copy and complete the table using the rust prevention methods given in the box.

sacrificial protection	galvanising	painting
oiling and greasing	electroplating	

Method of rust prevention	Description
	Used for moving parts of machinery and forms a protective film. Must be repeated to continue the protection.
	Used on cars. Uses a more reactive metal to coat the object and strong protection even if the metal layer is scratched.
	Used for small items and requires electricity.
	Used for ships, bridges and gates. Must be repeated to continue the protection.
	Used for oil rigs and hulls of ships. Uses blocks of reactive metal that are attached to iron surface.

2   Iron reacts with water and oxygen to form rust. Rusting is corrosion.

   a   Write **one** other factor that could increase the rate of corrosion.   [1]

   b   Aluminium is more reactive than iron. Explain why aluminium
       does not corrode in a damaging way as iron does.   [2]

   c   Suggest why rusting is a problem.   [2]

   [Total: 5]

3   Painting is **one** barrier method that can be used to protect iron and steel
    from rusting.

   a   State **one** other method of rust prevention.   [1]

   b   Describe how the method mentioned in **3a** helps to prevent rust.   [1]

   [Total: 2]

UNDERSTAND THESE TERMS
• galvanising
• rusting
• sacrificial protection

≪ RECALL AND CONNECT 2 ≪

Iron reacts with water and oxygen to form hydrated iron(III) oxide, which is also
known as rust. What products are formed when iron reacts with hydrochloric acid?

REFLECTION

How did you find the discuss question in this chapter? Do you feel confident that you understand what each command word means and how to approach a question that contains this command word?

Which areas do you feel you did well in throughout this chapter? Are there any areas you feel you need more practice in? The self-assessment checklist will help you to identify these areas.

You can test yourself by writing down the steps required to extract iron and aluminium from its ore. How will you check that you have increased your understanding? For example, are you confident you can explain how sacrificial protection prevents rust?

SELF-ASSESSMENT CHECKLIST

Let's revisit the Knowledge focus and Exam skills focus for this chapter.

Decide how confident you are with each statement.

Now I can:	Show it	Needs more work	Almost there	Confident to move on
consider the methods of extraction of metals from their ores in the context of the reactivity series of metals	Identify which metals are extracted using electrolysis and which metals are extracted using reduction by carbon.			
describe how moderately reactive metals can be extracted by reduction with carbon in a blast furnace, while reactive metals are extracted by electrolysis	List the metals in the reactivity series and show the position of carbon in the reactivity series.			
describe how iron is extracted from hematite in a blast furnace	Write down the steps required to extract iron from its ore.			
describe how aluminium is extracted from bauxite by the electrolysis of molten aluminium oxide	Write down the steps required to extract aluminium from its ore.			
discuss the causes of rusting and describe some barrier methods of rust prevention	List the reactants that react with iron to form rust and barrier prevention methods.			

CONTINUED

Now I can:	Show it	Needs more work	Almost there	Confident to move on
consider the chemistry of the extraction of iron	Write the word equation for the reactions that take place during the extraction of iron.			
describe the extraction of aluminium from bauxite	List the reactants added into the electrolytic cell to extract aluminium.			
consider galvanisation and sacrificial protection as methods of rust prevention.	Write down how galvanisation and sacrificial protection help prevent rust.			

17 Chemistry of our environment

KNOWLEDGE FOCUS

In this chapter you will answer questions on:

- air quality
- carbon dioxide, methane and climate change
- water.

EXAM SKILLS FOCUS

In this chapter you will:

- show that you understand the 'state' command word and can answer 'state' questions.

In this chapter you will answer questions with the command word 'state'. You will gain an understanding of how the answers to this type of question should be presented.

State	express in clear terms.

You are not expected to provide detailed explanations or descriptions for this command word. It is often combined with another question using a different command word, such as 'explain' or 'describe'. When you come across questions with two command words make sure you understand what is required for both, and the reasons for different marks available.

The command word 'state' was also a focus in Chapter 10 so you can revisit that chapter for further practice.

17.1 Air quality

1   Copy and complete the table giving the composition of clean dry air.
    Label these gases with their percentage:

type of gas	oxygen	other gases	nitrogen	carbon dioxide	argon
composition of clean dry air (%)					

2   Copy and complete the paragraph about the common air pollutants and their
    adverse effects. Fill in the blanks using words from the list in the box.

climate change	incomplete	sulfur dioxide	oxygen
photochemical smog	human activities	vehicles	particulates

Air pollutants are harmful substances and are often produced through

....

These pollutants include carbon dioxide and methane which are greenhouse gases
and contribute to ....

.... is another pollutant gas produced through the presence
of sulfur as an impurity in fossil fuels. This gas can contribute to respiratory
disease and cause acid rain.

Another pollutant that can cause acid rain are oxides of nitrogen. These gases
can be released through the emissions of some .... and cause
the formation of ....

Carbon monoxide is another pollutant that is produced from the ....
combustion of fuel, which occurs when there is a lack of ....
entering the engine.

3   Carbon monoxide is an example of an air pollutant.

   a   State **one** source of carbon monoxide.   [1]

   b   State **one** effect of carbon monoxide in humans.   [1]

   c   Carbon dioxide can be produced from the same source of carbon
      monoxide. State the percentage of carbon dioxide in clean dry air.   [1]

[Total: 3]

UNDERSTAND THESE TERMS

- acid-base reaction
- acid rain
- atmosphere
- catalytic converter
- clean dry air
- climate change
- complete combustion
- desulfurisation
- global warming
- incomplete combustion
- inert
- particulates
- photochemical smog
- photosynthesis
- pollutants
- respiration

≪ RECALL AND CONNECT 1 ≪

The Earth's atmosphere contains approximately 21% oxygen. Oxygen can
react with another substance and attack iron to form rust. What is the name
of this reaction?

17.2 Carbon dioxide, methane and climate change

1   Figure 17.1 shows the processes through which greenhouse gases are produced and how they can lead to climate change. Complete the flowchart using the correct words to replace letters A to G.

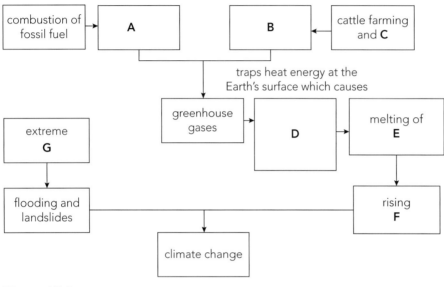

Figure 17.1

2   Greenhouse gases are gases that can absorb heat energy from the sun and trap the energy at the Earth's surface.

   a   State **two** of these greenhouse gases.   [2]
   b   State **one** effect of these greenhouse gases on the environment.   [1]
   c   Describe **three** methods to reduce emissions of greenhouse gases.   [3]

   [Total: 6]

3   Heat radiation from the Sun passes through Earth's atmosphere and reaches the Earth's surface. Greenhouse gases trap heat radiation in the atmosphere.

   a   Describe the characteristic of the radiation from the Sun and the radiation that is reflected back to the atmosphere in terms of energy.

      Radiation from the Sun:

      Radiation reflected back: [2]

   b   State **one** consequence of the absorption of the heat radiation by the Earth's surface.   [1]

   [Total: 3]

> **UNDERSTAND THESE TERMS**
>
> • chlorophyll
> • greenhouse effect
> • greenhouse gas
> • renewable (resources)

<< RECALL AND CONNECT 2 <<

Carbon dioxide is a greenhouse gas that contributes to the greenhouse effect. Carbon dioxide is also produced in a blast furnace during the extraction of iron from its ore. What is the substance that burns in a blast furnace to produce carbon dioxide?

17.3 Water

1   Water from natural sources contains dissolved substances that can either be beneficial or harmful. Arrange the dissolved substances from the list into the correct category to show which substances are beneficial and which are harmful.

| lead   nitrates   dissolved oxygen   sewage   iron   calcium salt |

Beneficial dissolved substances	Harmful dissolved substances

2   Arrange the following steps in the correct order to show the process of purification of domestic water. The first one has been done for you.

Water is moved to the sedimentation tank for soil and sand to sink and settle at the bottom.	
Water is then passed through sand filters to remove smaller insoluble particles.	
Small amounts of chlorine are added to water.	
Large rocks and plastics are removed from water through screening.	1
Water in the sedimentation tank is then treated with chlorine to disinfect the water.	
Dissolved organic compounds are then removed from water using carbon filters.	

3   Domestic water that has been purified is supplied to houses.

   a   State a chemical test for the presence of water and the results obtained.   [2]

   b   State the name of a substance used to remove dissolved organic compounds found in water during the purification of domestic water.   [1]

[Total: 3]

REFLECTION

How confident are you that you know what the command word 'state' means? Look back at your answers for the 'state' questions and make sure you have expressed your answer in clear terms.

What were the areas in this chapter that you felt most confident about? How will you check that you able to recall some of these concepts? For example, are you able to write a description of how greenhouse gases contribute to global warming and climate change? Can you think of a strategy to help you to recall this knowledge?

SELF-ASSESSMENT CHECKLIST

Let's revisit the Knowledge focus and Exam skills focus for this chapter.

Decide how confident you are with each statement.

Now I can:	Show it	Needs more work	Almost there	Confident to move on
describe how to describe the composition of clean dry air	Draw a labelled pie chart to show the percentages of different gases that make up the composition of clean dry air.			
investigate common air pollutants and their adverse effects	List the common air pollutants, their sources and their effects on humans and the environment.			
describe how carbon dioxide and methane are greenhouse gases linked to global warming and climate change	Write a flow chart to show how carbon dioxide and methane contribute to the greenhouse effect, global warming and climate change.			
describe and state the photosynthesis reaction	Write down the reactants and products in the process of photosynthesis.			
describe the tests for the presence and purity of water and why distilled water is used in experiments	List the tests used to detect the presence of water and their results. Write a paragraph explaining why distilled water is used in experiments.			

CONTINUED

Now I can:	Show it	Needs more work	Almost there	Confident to move on
discuss the sources of substances in water from natural sources and outline their impacts on human health and the environment	List the substances found in water that are beneficial and those substances that are harmful.			
describe the main steps needed to purify the domestic water supply	Write out the steps in water purification process in the correct order.			
explain how oxides of nitrogen form in car engines and are removed by catalytic converters	Write out the balanced symbol equations showing how oxides of nitrogen are formed and how they are removed in the catalytic convertor.			
understand how greenhouse gases cause global warming	Create a flowchart to show how greenhouse gases cause global warming.			
state the symbol equation for photosynthesis	Write out a balanced symbol equation for the photosynthesis reaction.			
understand the 'state' command word and answer 'state' questions.	Look at the Exam skills questions in this chapter and say why the command word 'state' was used in each of them.			

Exam practice 5

This section contains past paper questions from previous Cambridge exams, which draw together your knowledge on a range of topics that you have covered up to this point. These questions give you the opportunity to test your knowledge and understanding. Additional past paper practice questions can be found in the accompanying digital material.

The following question has an example student response and commentary provided. Once you have worked through the question, read the student response and commentary. Are your answers different to the sample answers?

1   This question is about aluminium.

a   The changes of state of aluminium are shown.

Name the changes of state represented by **A** and **B**.   [2]

b   Use the kinetic particle model to describe the differences between solid aluminium and liquid aluminium in terms of:

•   the arrangement of the particles

•   the separation of the particles.   [4]

c   Aluminium ore contains aluminium oxide.

i   Name the main ore of aluminium.   [1]

ii   Aluminium is extracted from aluminium oxide by electrolysis. Explain why aluminium is extracted by electrolysis and not by reduction with carbon.   [1]

d   Aluminium can be used to reduce iron(III) oxide to iron.

$$Fe_2O_3 + 2Al \rightarrow 2Fe + Al_2O_3$$

Describe how this equation shows that iron(III) oxide is reduced.   [1]

e   Aluminium is used for electric cables. State one **other** use of aluminium. Give a reason for this use in terms of the properties of aluminium.   [2]

f   Deduce the electronic structure of aluminium. Use the Periodic Table to help you.   [1]

[Total: 12]

Cambridge IGCSE Chemistry (0620) Paper 32, Q5 June 2022

Example student response	Commentary
1 a A – melting B – condensation	The student's response showed a strong recall of the changes of states of matter. ***This answer is awarded 2 out of 2 marks.***
b arrangement – particles are arranged more closely together separation – particles are closer together touching each other	The student's response showed a slight lack of skill in answering questions that address differences. Neither of the answers for arrangement and separation indicate clearly if the statement was referring to a solid or liquid. ***This answer is awarded 0 out of 4 marks.***
c i bauxite	The student showed a good recall of the name. ***This answer is awarded 1 out of 1 mark.***
ii too reactive	In a similar way to Question b, it would have been better if the response indicated clearly that this statement is referring to aluminium. However, one mark is awarded here because there is no comparison made, hence, the answer would be accepted here. ***This answer is awarded 1 out of 1 mark.***
d iron oxide loses oxygen	The student has demonstrated strong application skills by applying their understanding of the reduction concept to the equation and providing an explanation for this. ***This answer is awarded 1 out of 1 mark.***
e uses: aeroplane properties: good conductor of heat	This student demonstrated good recall of the uses of aluminium here. Hence, one mark is awarded here. However, the properties provided here do not relate to the uses correctly. Thus, no mark is awarded here. ***This answer is awarded 1 out of 2 marks.***
f 2, 8, 3	The student was able to correctly identify the electronic configuration. ***This answer is awarded 1 out of 1 mark.***

The student failed to answer Question b correctly in the above example due to misinterpreting the question. Answer the question correctly, keeping in mind the guidance given in the commentary.

The following question has an example student response and commentary provided.

Once you have worked through the question, compare your answer to the student response and commentary.

2 This question is about cobalt and its compounds.

a A coloured crystal of cobalt(II) chloride was placed at the bottom of a beaker containing water. After 2 days, the colour had spread throughout the water.

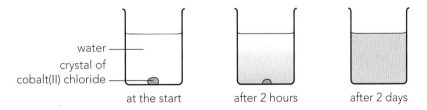

water —
crystal of
cobalt(II) chloride —

at the start   after 2 hours   after 2 days

Explain these observations using the kinetic particle model. [3]

b Cobalt(II) chloride can be used to test for the presence of water.

$$CoCl_2 + 6H_2O \rightleftharpoons CoCl_2.6H_2O$$

        anhydrous   hydrated

        cobalt(II) chloride   cobalt(II) chloride

  i   What is meant by the symbol $\rightleftharpoons$?   [1]

  ii Describe how the colour of anhydrous cobalt(II) chloride changes
      when water is added to it.   [2]

      from .... to ....

c A compound of cobalt can be represented by the structure shown.

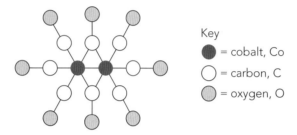

Key

● = cobalt, Co

○ = carbon, C

◉ = oxygen, O

  Deduce the molecular formula of this compound showing the number
  of cobalt, carbon and oxygen atoms.   [1]

d The table compares the reactivity of cobalt with that of three
  other metals.

metal	reactivity with cold water	reactivity with steam
barium	reacts rapidly	
cobalt	no reaction	reacts slowly when heated
magnesium	reacts very slowly	reacts rapidly
zinc	no reaction	reacts easily when heated

  Use this information to put the metals in order of their reactivity.
  Put the least reactive metal first.   [2]

e Cobalt is a transition element. Lithium is an element in Group I of the
  Periodic Table. Describe **three** ways in which the properties of cobalt
  differ from those of lithium.   [2]

f When cobalt(II) oxide, CoO, is heated in air, an oxide with the formula
  Co_3O_4 is formed. Balance the chemical equation for this reaction.   [1]

$$.....CoO + O_2 \rightarrow 2Co_3O_4$$

g When Co_3O_4 is heated with hydrogen, cobalt metal can be formed.

$$Co_3O_4 + 4H_2 \rightarrow 3Co + 4H_2O$$

  How does this equation show that Co_3O_4 is reduced?   [1]

                        [Total: 13]

Cambridge IGCSE Chemistry (0620) Paper 33, Q3 June 2018

Example student response	Commentary
2 a particles diffuse and spread out	The student's response showed a good understanding of kinetic particle model with the use of the term 'particles'. However, the student missed out an important term on the kinetic theory description, which is 'collision'. ***This answer is awarded 2 out of 3 marks.***
b i reversible	The response here showed that student recognised the arrow for the chemical reaction. ***This answer is awarded 1 out of 1 mark.***
ii from blue to pink	The student's response demonstrated a good knowledge recall of the test used for water and shows good understanding of the colour change. ***This answer is awarded 2 out of 2 marks.***
c $Co_2C_8O_8$ CoC_4O_4	The student's response showed good analytical skills where they extract information from the diagram and write down the molecular formula. However, the student also wrote the empirical formula, the simplified formula, whereas the question is asking for molecular formula instead. ***This answer is awarded 0 out of 1 mark.***
d cobalt<zinc<magnesium <barium	The response here showed that the student was able to analyse the information from the table and arrange the metals in increasing reactivity. ***This answer is awarded 2 out of 2 marks.***
e boiling point, density, cobalt forms coloured compounds	The response showed good knowledge recall of the properties of transition elements compared to Group I elements. However, the response is slightly weak because indicating the properties 'boiling point' and 'density' does not show the difference between cobalt and lithium. Hence, only one mark is awarded here for the property on cobalt forming coloured compounds. ***This answer is awarded 1 out of 3 marks.***
f $6CoO + O_2 \rightarrow 2Co_3O_4$	The response here showed that the student has good skills in balancing equations as the number of Co atoms are balanced in the equation. ***This answer is awarded 1 out of 1 mark.***
g gaining of electrons	This student shows knowledge recall of what a reduction reaction is. However, the mistake here is that the student did not address the part of the question which is asking them to refer to the equation. The equation shows that it is a reduction reaction because of the oxygen. ***This answer is awarded 0 out of 1 mark.***

3 Now that you've gone through the commentary to the previous question, have a go at writing a full mark scheme for this question. This will check that you've understood why each mark has (or has not) been allocated. The more often you do this, and the better you get to know the way mark schemes are written, the more confident you will feel about your answers to these questions.

The following question has an example student response and commentary provided. Once you have worked through the question, compare your answer to the student response and commentary. Do you feel that you need to improve your understanding of this topic?

4   The diagram shows a blast furnace used in the extraction of iron.

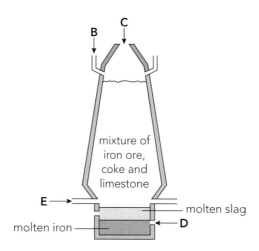

a   i   Complete the chemical equation for the reduction of iron(III) oxide in the blast furnace.   [2]

$$Fe_2O_3 + 3C \rightarrow ......Fe + ...CO$$

ii   Explain how this equation shows that iron(III) oxide is reduced.   [1]

b   Calcium carbonate (limestone) is added to the blast furnace. The calcium carbonate undergoes thermal decomposition.

i   Complete the word equation for this reaction.   [2]

ii   One of the products of this reaction reacts with impurities in the iron to form slag.

Use the information in the diagram to suggest how you know that molten slag is less dense than molten iron.   [1]

c   i   Use words from the list to complete these sentences about how steel is made from iron.

**acidic   basic   chlorides   methane   neutral
nitrogen   oxides   oxygen   sulfates**

A gas is blown through the molten iron. The name of this gas is .... Acidic gases are formed. These acidic gases react with ....   [3]

    ii   State **one** use of mild steel. [1]

    iii   Metals such as chromium are added to iron to make stainless steel. The symbol for an isotope of chromium is shown.

$$^{53}_{24}\text{Cr}$$

        Deduce the number of electrons, neutrons and protons in one atom of this isotope of chromium.

        number of electrons:
        number of neutrons:
        number of protons: [3]

d   Chromium conducts electricity and is shiny. Give **two** other physical properties of chromium that are characteristic of all metals. [2]

[Total: 15]

Cambridge IGCSE Chemistry (0620) Paper 31, Q3b, c, d November 2021

Example student response	Commentary
4 **a** **i** $Fe_2O_3 + 3CO \rightarrow$ **2**Fe **+ 3**CO$_2$	The student demonstrated good skills in balancing chemical equations and managed to add the correct numbers to balance the equation. **This answer is awarded 2 out of 2 marks.**
ii loss of oxygen	The student's response demonstrated a good knowledge recall of the meaning of reduction. **This answer is awarded 1 out of 1 mark.**
b **i** calcium carbonate $\rightarrow$ **calcium oxide + carbon dioxide**	The student demonstrated good knowledge recall of the products produced when calcium carbonate decomposes. **This answer is awarded 2 out of 2 marks.**
ii molten slag is found above the molten iron	The student was able to analyse the diagram correctly and extract information or evidence to indicate that slag is less dense than iron. **This answer is awarded 1 out of 1 mark.**
c **i** A gas is blown through the molten iron. The name of this gas is **oxygen**. Acidic gases are formed. These acidic gases react with **basic oxides.**	The response demonstrated good knowledge recall of the acid base reactions for oxides. The student was able to name the gases and oxide terms correctly. **This answer is awarded 3 out of 3 marks.**
ii car bodies	The response here showed that the student was able to list one use of stainless steel. **This answer is awarded 1 out of 1 mark.**

CAMBRIDGE IGCSE CHEMISTRY: EXAM PREPARATION AND PRACTICE

Example student response	Commentary
iii electrons – 24 neutrons – 29 protons – 24	The student showed good knowledge recall and application skills by firstly indicating a correct number of electrons. This showed that the student understands the command term 'deduce' as well as being able to indicate that the number of protons is equal to number of electrons. Hence, two marks are awarded here for correct number of electrons and protons. The student also demonstrated good application skills by giving the correct number of neutrons and being able to recall that the number of neutrons is obtained by subtracting the atomic number or proton number from the mass number. Hence, one mark is gained here. ***This answer is awarded 3 out of 3 marks.***
d good conductor of heat malleable	The student demonstrated good knowledge recall of the physical properties of metals. ***This answer is awarded 2 out of 2 marks.***

Now that you've gone through the commentary to the previous question, try another similar question.

5 Lime (calcium oxide) is made by heating limestone (calcium carbonate).

$$CaCO_3(s) \rightleftharpoons CaO(s) + CO_2(g)$$

   a **i**   Is this reaction exothermic or endothermic? Explain your answer.   [1]

        ii The reaction is reversible. What information in the equation shows that this reaction is reversible?   [1]

   b Explain why farmers use lime to treat acidic soils.   [2]

   c Limestone is used to manufacture cement. The limestone is mixed with clay and heated to 1500 °C. It is then mixed with calcium sulfate and crushed.

        i   Describe the test for sulfate ions.

           test:
           result: [2]

        ii Concrete is a mixture of cement, silicates and water.
Part of the structure of a silicate is shown.

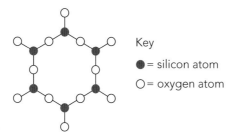

Key
● = silicon atom
○ = oxygen atom

           Deduce the molecular formula for this silicate.   [1]

d Concrete contains small amounts of calcium oxide.
This can react with rainwater to form calcium hydroxide.

    i Calcium hydroxide is strongly alkaline.

    What is the most likely pH of a strongly alkaline solution?
Draw a ring around the correct answer. [1]

        pH 2   pH 6   pH 7   pH 12

    ii The calcium hydroxide on the surface of a piece of concrete reacts
with carbon dioxide in the air. Complete the chemical equation for
this reaction. [1]

$$Ca(OH)_2 + CO_2 \rightarrow CaCO_3 + \text{................}$$

    iii Limewater is an aqueous solution of calcium hydroxide. A teacher left
an open beaker of limewater in the laboratory. After a week, the solution
in the beaker was pH 7 and a white precipitate was observed.

    Use the information in **d i** and **d ii** to help you explain
these observations. [3]

[Total: 12]

*Adapted from Cambridge IGCSE Chemistry (0620) Paper 33, Q5 a, c, d, e
November 2016*

The following question has an example student response and commentary provided.
Work through the question first, then compare your answer to the sample response
and commentary. Did you make any of the same mistakes?

6 **a** The table shows the percentage by volume of each of the gases present
in the exhaust gases from a petrol engine and a diesel engine.

name	percentage by volume from a petrol engine	percentage by volume from a diesel engine
nitrogen	72.00	67.00
carbon dioxide	14.00	
water vapor	12.00	11.00
carbon monoxide	1.50	0.05
oxides of nitrogen	0.25	0.70
hydrocarbons	0.24	0.22
sulfur dioxide	0.01	0.03
oxygen	0.00	9.00
total	100.00	total	100.00

    i In the diesel engine, nitrogen, carbon dioxide and water vapour account
for 90.00% of the exhaust gases by volume. Calculate the percentage by
volume of carbon dioxide in the exhaust gases from the diesel engine. [1]

    ii Describe **three** ways in which the composition of the exhaust gases from the petrol engine differ from the composition of the exhaust gases from the diesel engine. [3]

        1.

        2.

        3.

    iii Give **one** adverse effect of sulfur dioxide on health. [1]

b Complete the sentences about the separation of petroleum into fractions using words from the list.

    boiling   crystallisation   density   distillation   kerosene   poly(ethene)

    Fractional .... of petroleum produces fractions such as gasoline, diesel oil and .... Within each fraction, the molecules have a particular range of .... points. [3]

c Balance the chemical equation for the complete combustion of propane. [2]

$$C_3H_8 + 5O_2 \rightarrow \text{.....}CO_2 + \text{.....}H_2O$$

[Total: 10]

Cambridge IGCSE Chemistry (0620) Paper 33, Q2 June 2018

Example student response	Commentary
6 **a** **i** $100 - (67 + 11 + 0.05 + 0.7 + 0.22 + 0.03 + 9)$ $= 12\%$	The student's response demonstrated good analytical and calculation skills. The student was able to analyse the data from the table and apply mathematical skills of finding the percentage of carbon dioxide by subtracting the percentage of other gases from the total of 100%. ***This answer is awarded 1 out of 1 mark.***
ii nitrogen, oxides of nitrogen, oxygen	The student was able to indicate that the composition of gases in a petrol engine and a diesel engine is different. However, the response is slightly weak and lacking in the description that would show the differences or comparison. Words such as 'more' or 'less' should be used when making comparisons. ***This answer is awarded 0 out of 3 marks.***
iii acid rain	The response here showed a common careless mistake in which the student did not read the question properly. The question here specified effect on health and not environment or in general. Only indicating acid rain does not show if the effect is on health or environment. ***This answer is awarded 0 out of 1 mark.***
b distillation, kerosene, boiling	The response here showed good knowledge recall of the right separation method used for hydrocarbons. ***This answer is awarded 3 out of 3 marks.***
c $C_3H_8 + 5O_2 \rightarrow \textbf{3}CO_2 + \textbf{4}H_2O$	The student demonstrated good skills in balancing symbol equations. Both the coefficient numbers given are correct. ***This answer is awarded 2 out of 2 marks.***

7 Now that you've gone through the commentary to the previous question, try to write an improved answer to the parts where you dropped marks. This will check if you've understood exactly why each mark has (or has not) been allocated.

18 Introduction to organic chemistry

KNOWLEDGE FOCUS

In this chapter you will answer questions on:

- names and formulae of organic compounds

> structural formulae, homologous series and isomerism.

EXAM SKILLS FOCUS

In this chapter you will:

- practise distinguishing instructional text, such as 'draw', from command words.

Exam questions may include additional instructional text in addition to command words. One example is the word 'draw'. Drawing diagrams, formulae or molecules to show the information asked for by the questions is a skill you need to practise. In this chapter you will practise answering questions containing the word 'draw'.

18.1 Names and formulae of organic compounds

1 What is the general formula for each of the following?

a alkanes

b alkenes

c alcohols

UNDERSTAND THESE TERMS

- alkanes
- hydrocarbons
- organic chemistry
- saturated hydrocarbons

2 Copy and complete the table to show how organic compounds are named according to their functional group and the number of carbon atoms they contain.

Number of carbons	Prefix	Alkane		Alkene	
		Name	Formula	Name	Formula
1				–	–
2					
3					
4					
5					
6					

UNDERSTAND THESE TERMS

- displayed formula
- molecular formula

3 State the name of the carboxylic acid containing two carbon atoms and draw its displayed formula. **[Total: 2]**

4 Explain why there is no alkene called methene. **[Total: 3]**

« RECALL AND CONNECT 1 «

Draw a dot-and-cross diagram to show the covalent bonding in ethanoic acid.

UNDERSTAND THESE TERMS

- addition reaction
- alkenes
- unsaturated hydrocarbon

18.2 Structural formulae, homologous series and isomerism

UNDERSTAND THESE TERMS

- homologous series
- functional group

1 Give the molecular, structural and displayed formulae of ethanol and describe the differences between them.

2 Draw the displayed formula for a structural isomer of each of these molecules:

a

```
    H   H   H   H
    |   |   |   |
H — C — C — C — C — H
    |   |   |   |
    H   H   H   H
```

b

```
 H      H   H   H
  \     |   |   |
   C = C — C — C — H
  /         |   |
 H          H   H
```

c

```
    H   H   H   H
    |   |   |   |
H — C — C — C — C — O — H
    |   |   |   |
    H   H   H   H
```

3 Describe and explain the trend in boiling point of the alkanes as the number of carbon atoms in the molecule increases.   **[Total: 3]**

≪ **RECALL AND CONNECT 2** ≪

Why are simple covalent compounds often liquids or gases at room temperature?

REFLECTION

Organic chemistry involves lots of lateral thinking compared to other areas of chemistry.

What strategies are you using to organise your notes and your thinking so that you can answer different questions on this topic? Were you able to see the connections between topics in this chapter? Check your answers against those provided – did you successfully demonstrate the required knowledge?

UNDERSTAND THESE TERMS

- esters
- intermolecular forces
- structural formula
- structural isomerism

SELF-ASSESSMENT CHECKLIST

Let's revisit the Knowledge focus and Exam skills focus for this chapter.

Decide how confident you are with each statement.

Now I can:	Show it	Needs more work	Almost there	Confident to move on
describe how a homologous series of organic compounds has the same general formula and similar chemical properties	Make a mind map of the four homologous series you have learned about, summarising their similarities.			
state that the alkanes are a series of saturated hydrocarbons as all the carbon–carbon bonds are single covalent bonds	Explain what the term saturated means and draw the displayed formulae of two alkanes as examples to show the meaning.			
understand that compounds containing at least one carbon–carbon double or triple bond are unsaturated molecules	Explain what the term unsaturated means and draw the displayed formulae of two alkenes as examples to show the meaning.			
distinguish between saturated and unsaturated molecules by testing	Draw a labelled diagram of the test-tube reactions of an alkane and an alkene with aqueous bromine. Write down how you would do this test step-by-step.			
describe how alcohols and carboxylic acids are further homologous series and that the type of organic compound present is given a systematic name	Name the first four alcohols and carboxylic acids, and draw their displayed formulae.			
distinguish the different organic compounds by their molecular and displayed formulae	Write the molecular formula, and draw the displayed formula beside it, of the molecule with two carbon atoms in each of the four functional groups you have learned about.			

CONTINUED

Now I can:	Show it	Needs more work	Almost there	Confident to move on
understand how to write the structural formulae of molecules from various homologous series	Write structural formulae beside your displayed and molecular formulae of the molecule with two carbon atoms in each of the four functional groups you have learned about. Draw the displayed formula and write the molecular and structural formulae of the ester that would be formed from the alcohol and carboxylic acid you have drawn.			
define structural isomers	Write down the definition of isomers without copying it.			
describe the general characteristics of a homologous series	Check to make sure you have included increasing chain length, similar chemical properties and related trends in physical properties on your homologous series mind map. If not, add them.			
understand how to draw different formulae of unbranched members of different homologous series	Play a game with a die. Throw the die and draw the structural and displayed formulae of the molecule that contains the same number of carbon atoms as shown on the upward face of the die. If you throw a 5 or a 6, draw an ester with that number of carbon atoms. Identify the alcohol and the carboxylic acid that would make the ester you have drawn.			
distinguish instructional text, such as 'draw', from command words.	Look through the practice exam questions and find any that contain the word 'draw'. Look at the mark schemes to find out how many marks are awarded for the 'draw' part of the question.			

19 Reactions of organic compounds

As you work through this chapter, look for the question that asks you to compare two methods, and the marks allocated. Think about what points you need to make, how much detail you need to include and which key terms you need to use in your answer. You can then check your answer against the answer provided to see how the marks are broken down.

19.1 Characteristic reactions of different homologous series

1 Name **two** types of reaction that alkanes undergo.

2 What products are formed when alkanes burn in
   a a good supply of oxygen?
   b a limited supply of oxygen?

3 Name the process that produces alkenes from long-chain alkanes.

4 What type of reactions do alkenes undergo?

5 Why is there no substitution reaction between an alkane and chlorine in the dark?

6 Copy and complete the table to show how ethene reacts in addition reactions with different reactants and conditions.

Reactant	Reagent	Conditions	Displayed formula of product
bromine	$Br_2(l)$	normal conditions	
bromine	$Br_2(aq)$	normal conditions	
hydrogen		150–300 °C, nickel catalyst	
water	$H_2O(g)$		

7 Describe the substitution reaction between ethane and chlorine and give a word equation for the reaction. **[Total: 3]**

8 Describe a chemical test you could use to distinguish between hexane and hexene. Describe the observations you would expect to make in each case. **[Total: 3]**

« RECALL AND CONNECT 1 «

Name and draw the displayed formula of the first four alkanes.

UNDERSTAND THESE TERMS

- catalytic cracking
- fractional distillation
- hydration
- hydrogenation
- isomers
- photochemical reaction
- substitution reaction

19.2 Chemistry of ethanol

1 Describe the two different methods that can be used to produce ethanol.

2 Write a balanced symbol equation for the combustion of ethanol. Include state symbols.

3 Ethanol can be produced on an industrial scale by hydration of ethene or by fermentation. Describe four features of the hydration of ethene method, and compare each feature with the fermentation method.

[Total: 4]

> UNDERSTAND
> THESE TERMS
> - alcohols
> - fermentation

REFLECTION

How confident are you when a question asks you to 'compare'? Did you score all four marks in Exam skill Question 3? Can you explain what is required in an answer to a 'compare' question?

19.3 Carboxylic acids and esters

1 Draw the displayed formula for the functional group present in carboxylic acids.

2 Ethyl ethanoate is made by reacting ethanol and ethanoic acid in the presence of sulfuric acid. Figure 19.1 shows the displayed formula of ethyl ethanoate.

   a Circle the molecule's functional group on Figure 19.1.

   b What is the name of this functional group?

   c What are some uses of this type of compound?

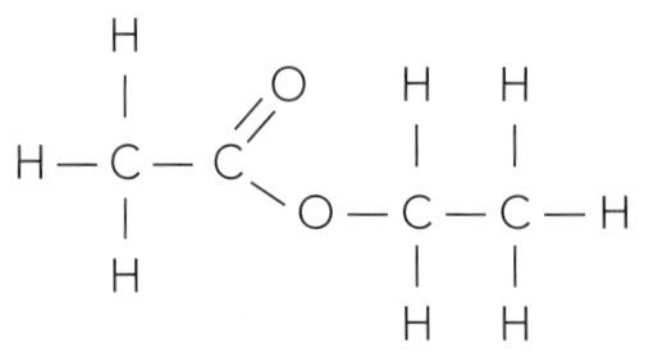

Figure 19.1: Ethyl ethanoate

« RECALL AND CONNECT 2 «

Acids characteristically react with metals, bases and carbonates. Name the products of the reactions of hydrochloric acid with:

a magnesium

b sodium hydroxide

c calcium carbonate.

> UNDERSTAND
> THESE TERMS
> - carboxylic acids
> - esterification

3 Write a balanced symbol equation for the reaction of ethanoic acid with sodium carbonate.

[Total: 2]

REFLECTION

Devising a chart of reactions can be a helpful tool to organise your overall understanding of a topic. How can you go further with your chart to help you to remember them?

(**Hint:** think – look, cover, write, check.) How might turning your chart into a learning game make it easier for you to memorise them?

SELF-ASSESSMENT CHECKLIST

Let's revisit the Knowledge focus and Exam skills focus for this chapter.

Decide how confident you are with each statement.

Now I can:	Show it	Needs more work	Almost there	Confident to move on
describe the alkanes as a series of generally unreactive compounds that burn readily and undergo substitution reactions with chlorine	List two types of reaction that alkanes undergo.			
understand that alkenes can be obtained by catalytic cracking	Describe the conditions for catalytic cracking and name the types of products obtained from it.			
understand that ethanol is manufactured either by fermentation or by the catalytic hydration of ethene, and that it can be used as a solvent and as a fuel	Make a table comparing the manufacture of ethanol by fermentation and catalytic hydration of ethene.			
describe the reactions of ethanoic acid with metals, bases and metal carbonates	Identify the products of the reaction of ethanoic acid with a metal, a metal hydroxide and a metal carbonate.			
understand that the substitution reactions of alkanes with chlorine are photochemical reactions	Define the terms substitution reaction and photochemical reaction.			

CONTINUED

Now I can:	Show it	Needs more work	Almost there	Confident to move on
describe how alkenes take part in addition reactions	Define the term addition reaction and draw displayed formula for the products of bromination, hydrogenation and hydration of ethene.			
understand the advantages and disadvantages of the two methods of manufacturing ethanol	In your table on ethanol manufacture, identify the advantages and disadvantages of each method of ethanol production by highlighting each in two different colours.			
understand how ethanoic acid can be formed by the oxidation of ethanol	Write an equation to show how ethanoic acid is obtained from ethanol.			
describe the reaction of a carboxylic acid and an alcohol to form an ester	Give the conditions needed for an alcohol and a carboxylic acid to react and identify the ester functional group in the product molecule.			
understand how to answer questions that ask you to 'compare'.	Write a question of your own that requires you to compare two things, such as two methods, and allocate marks.			

20 Petrochemicals and polymers

KNOWLEDGE FOCUS

In this chapter you will answer questions on:

- petroleum and its products
- polymers
- plastics.

EXAM SKILLS FOCUS

In this chapter you will:

- show that you know what a good response looks like and practise and improve your answers.

To provide an appropriate response to an exam question it is important to be aware of what might be expected in the mark scheme. Use PEA (point, evidence, analyse) or PEE (point, evidence, explain) to make sure your response has specific evidence or examples. Check your answers to the exam skill questions in this chapter against those provided and practise improving your responses.

20.1 Petroleum and its products

1   Describe the relationship between the length of a hydrocarbon chain and each
    of the following properties:

    a   boiling point

    b   viscosity

    c   volatility.

2   Draw lines to match each fraction from fractional distillation of crude oil to its
    use. The first one has been done for you.

Fraction	Use
paraffin (kerosene)	chemical feedstock
petrol (gasoline)	ships and home heating
naphtha	bottled gas for heating and cooking
fuel oil	fuel in diesel engines
bitumen	fuel in jet engines and as heating oil
refinery gas	waxes and polishes
lubricating oil	surfacing roads
diesel oil	fuel in cars

3   Describe how the process of fractional distillation is used to separate
    hydrocarbons with different chain lengths in petroleum.   **[Total: 4]**

≪ RECALL AND CONNECT 1 ≪

Write an equation to represent the cracking of paraffin ($C_{16}H_{34}$) to form
a molecule used for petrol (C_8H_{18}) and four molecules of an alkene.

REFLECTION

Fractional distillation of crude oil produces fractions with different hydrocarbon
chain lengths. If you write the names of the fractions on one set of revision cards
and the uses of the fractions on another set, what games might you play to help
you to link each fraction with its use?

UNDERSTAND THESE TERMS

- chemical feedstock
- coal
- fossil fuels
- natural gas
- non-renewable (finite) resource
- petroleum (crude oil)

20.2 Polymers

1 Ethene monomers join together in an addition polymerisation reaction to form poly(ethene). Draw a section of poly(ethene) formed from the four monomers drawn in Figure 20.1.

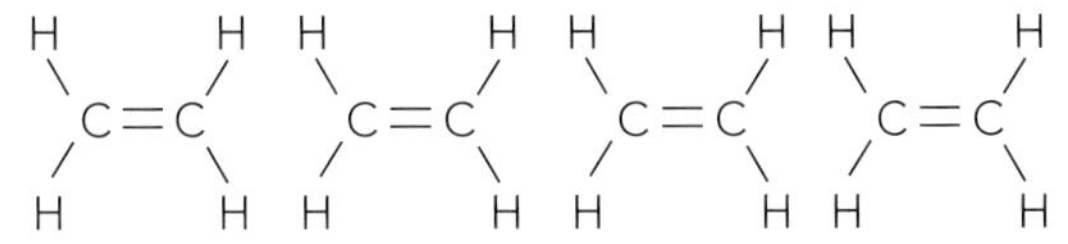

Figure 20.1: Ethene monomers

2 Poly(phenylethene), or poly(styrene), is an addition polymer used for insulation and packaging. A section of the polymer chain is given in Figure 20.2.

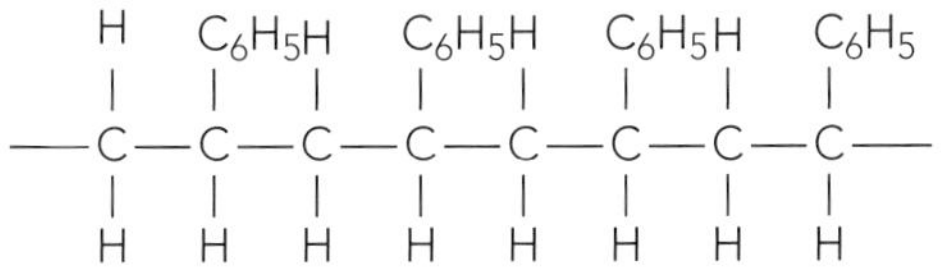

Figure 20.2: Section of poly(phenylethene)

a Identify and draw the repeat unit in poly(phenylethene).

b Draw and name the monomer used to make poly(phenylethene).

3 Describe the processes of addition and condensation polymerisation. **[Total: 4]**

UNDERSTAND THESE TERMS

- addition polymer
- amino acids
- monomer
- polymer
- polymerisation
- proteins

UNDERSTAND THESE TERMS

- amide link (peptide link)
- condensation polymer
- condensation reaction
- polyamide
- polyester

20.3 Plastics

1 a List **three** ways in which we can adapt our use of plastics in the light of the environmental challenges we face.

b What problems are associated with:

i disposal of plastics in landfill sites

ii incineration of plastic waste?

2 Describe how PET can be recycled.

3 Explain why recycling of plastics is not always easy. **[Total: 3]**

« RECALL AND CONNECT 2 «

Describe some problems caused by different types of plastics in the oceans.

UNDERSTAND THESE TERMS

- hydrolysis
- microplastics
- plastics

REFLECTION

PEE (point, evidence, explain) or PEA (point, evidence, analyse) are useful tools to use when constructing written responses to questions that demand specific detail.

How can you organise your notes on the environmental issues surrounding the use of plastics to ensure that you can provide specific examples and evidence to illustrate any points you might want to make?

SELF-ASSESSMENT CHECKLIST

Let's revisit the Knowledge focus and Exam skills focus for this chapter.

Decide how confident you are with each statement.

Now I can:	Show it	Needs more work	Almost there	Confident to move on
describe how the major fossil fuels are coal, natural gas and petroleum	Draw a labelled diagram to illustrate how coal, oil and gas were formed.			
describe how fractional distillation can be used to separate petroleum into a range of fractions	Make a flowchart summarising the key steps in fractional distillation.			
define polymers as long-chain molecules built up from smaller molecules (monomers)	Draw, or make with beads, different polymers using only one, two or several different beads. Label your drawing or describe your model to someone else.			
describe how plastics are made from synthetic polymers	Make a word cloud using the words synthetic polymer and plastic, with other associated words.			
describe the environmental challenges posed by plastics	List the environmental problems with plastics and give three bullet points outlining more details for each one.			
identify the structure of an addition polymer or its repeat unit	Look up the structure of Teflon (PTFE) and draw the structures of its repeat unit and the monomer used to make it.			

CONTINUED

Now I can:	Show it	Needs more work	Almost there	Confident to move on
understand that polymers can also be formed by condensation reactions	Explain what a condensation reaction is and name a polymer that is made this way.			
identify the structure of a condensation polymer or its repeat unit from given monomers	Look up the structure of terylene and draw the structures of the monomers used to make it.			
describe the differences between addition and condensation polymerisation	Make a Venn diagram comparing addition and condensation polymers.			
describe proteins as natural condensation polyamides, and describe the general structure of amino acids and proteins	Look up the structures of three amino acids and highlight their common features. Draw a diagram to show how they might join to form part of a protein and label the amide (peptide) link.			
know what a good response looks like and practise and improve my answers.	Write improved answers to Question 5 a (ii) and (iii) and Question 11 a in Exam practice 6, making sure you give specific details.			

21 Experimental design and separation techniques

To understand what you are expected to include in an answer, it is important that you are familiar with mark schemes and the language of the syllabus. Make sure you understand how the marks are broken down across a question by checking how many marks are allocated to each part of the question. Check that your answers contain enough detail to score all the marks on offer.

21.1 Experimental design

1 Copy and complete the table with the correct apparatus for each purpose.

Apparatus	Purpose
	measure temperature of liquid
	measure a variable volume of liquid, can be used for titration
	measure a fixed volume of liquid, for example 10 cm^3 or 25 cm^3
	measure time for rate of reaction
	measure mass of solid

2 Copy and complete the table with the correct term for each definition.

Term	Definition
	How close a value is to the true value.
	Variable that is measured during a scientific investigation.
	Something that is unusual or unexpected and deviates from the normal. One of a series of repeated experimental results that is much larger or smaller than the others.
	The smallest division on the instrument.
	Where an experiment can be repeated using the same method to obtain similar results.

UNDERSTAND THESE TERMS

- accuracy
- anomalous
- dependent variable
- independent variable
- precision

3 A student is trying to measure the mass of calcium carbonate powder. However, the student noticed that the apparatus is showing a mass reading when it should not.

a Identify **one** piece of apparatus that can be used to measure the mass of the powder. [1]

b Suggest the type of error that could have happened. [1]

[Total: 2]

21.2 Separation and purification

1 What separation technique could be used to obtain the following substances from each mixture?

a copper(II) oxide from copper(II) oxide and water

b copper(II) sulfate crystals from copper(II) sulfate solution

c individual dyes from a sample of ink

d water from sodium chloride solution

2 A mixture can be separated using different physical processes to produce a pure substance.

    a State the name of the process that is used to separate sand from water. [1]

    b Describe a method to determine the purity of the substance produced from a mixture. [2]

                           [Total: 3]

3 Seawater is a mixture.

    a State the name of the process that is used to obtain pure water from seawater. [1]

    b Describe how the process named in **a** is used to separate pure water from seawater. [2]

                           [Total: 3]

≪ RECALL AND CONNECT 1 ≪

Fractional distillation is the process used to separate hydrocarbons in crude oil. What property is used to separate crude oil into the different fractions (groups) of hydrocarbons?

21.3 Chromatography

1 Figure 21.1 shows the outline of a chromatogram.

Copy and complete Figure 21.1 adding each of the following labels in the correct positions.

solvent front	chromatography paper	solvent	baseline

2 Arrange the following steps in the correct order to show how the process of chromatography is carried out.

Place a drop of mixture solution on the baseline.	
Remove the chromatography paper from the solvent before the solvent front reaches the top of the paper.	
Dip the chromatography paper into the solvent with the level of the solvent below the baseline.	
Calculate the R_f value.	
Draw the baseline 1 cm up from the bottom edge of the chromatography paper using pencil.	1
Measure the distance travelled by the solvent front and the distance travelled by the sample drop.	
Allow the solvent to move up the chromatography paper.	

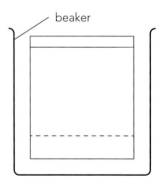

Figure 21.1: A partial chromatography set-up

UNDERSTAND THESE TERMS

- anti-bumping granules
- chromatography
- crystallisation
- desalination
- distillate
- filtrate
- filtration
- fractional distillation
- mixture
- pure substance
- residue
- simple distillation
- solution

3 Coloured dye is a mixture that consists of individual-coloured substances.

   a State the name of the method used to separate the substances in the coloured dye. [1]

   b Suggest a method that could be used to determine the identity of the individual substance separated from the coloured dye. [2]

[Total: 3]

UNDERSTAND THESE TERMS

- chromatogram
- locating agent
- paper chromatography
- R_f value
- solvent front

≪ RECALL AND CONNECT 2 ≪

Chromatography is found useful in the analysis of molecules such as amino acids. Amino acids are components that make up proteins. What is the type of polymerisation that occurs when amino acids join to form a protein?

REFLECTION

When completing the Exam skills questions, did you notice the marks available for each one? When you answered Question 2 in section 21.2 did you think about how to gain the two marks for part b? A two-mark answer to a 'describe' question should usually include two concepts or details.

Do you understand the difference between the command words 'state' and 'describe' and why they are allocated different numbers of marks?

SELF-ASSESSMENT CHECKLIST

Let's revisit the Knowledge focus and Exam skills focus for this chapter.

Decide how confident you are with each statement.

Now I can:	Show it	Needs more work	Almost there	Confident to move on
develop an understanding of experimental design	Create a flowchart to show the steps taken for an experimental design.			
describe how to select the most appropriate methods and apparatus to use in an experiment together with their possible advantages and disadvantages	Name the apparatus used for a given experiment and give the reasons they are being used.			
name appropriate apparatus for measuring different variables	Create a table which indicates the name of an apparatus, variables measured and measurement unit.			

CONTINUED

Now I can:	Show it	Needs more work	Almost there	Confident to move on
explore and identify techniques to separate and purify different substances	List different separation and purification techniques used for different types of mixtures.			
discover how melting and boiling points can be used to identify and assess the purity of a substance	Write out the steps used to test the purity of a substance.			
describe how chromatography can be used to separate mixtures of soluble coloured substances	Draw a labelled diagram of a paper chromatogram and annotate the diagram to indicate the steps in running paper chromatography.			
state and use the equation to determine the R_f value	Write out the equation used to calculate an R_f value and try one practice question.			
describe how paper chromatography can be used to separate mixtures of soluble colourless substances using a locating agent	List the steps in paper chromatography used to separate mixtures of soluble colourless substances and identify them using a locating agent.			
answer questions fully through paying attention to the mark schemes.	Practise Exam skills questions and compare your own answers to the written answers provided, identifying the total number of marks given for each key point.			

22 Chemical analysis

KNOWLEDGE FOCUS

In this chapter you will answer questions on:

- tests to identify common cations
- tests to identify common anions
- tests to identify common gases
- quantitative analysis: acid-base titrations.

EXAM SKILLS FOCUS

In this chapter you will:

- show that you understand the 'calculate' command word and can answer 'calculate' questions.

'Calculate' is a higher order thinking skill and there are opportunities in this chapter to practise. Take careful note of the process in your calculations and the numerical data you use. Show your working to make your thinking explicit.

| Calculate | work out from given facts, figures or information. |

The chemical tests presented in this chapter, both qualitative and quantitative, are studied explicitly here as a standalone topic but are used in real life in a wide range of different contexts. Some different contexts are offered here. Thinking about how these tests relate to topics you have already learned about will help you to remember both.

22.1 Tests to identify common cations

1 A sample taken from a solution containing metal ions produced a red flame during a flame test. A white precipitate was formed in the solution when a small amount of sodium hydroxide solution was added and this precipitate did not dissolve on further addition of sodium hydroxide.

What was the identity of the metal ions present in the solution?

2 How would you carry out a flame test to identify the metal cations in a salt?

3 a Give the balanced symbol equation, including state symbols, representing the reaction between copper(II) sulfate and sodium hydroxide. [3]

  b Describe what you would see during the initial reaction between copper(II) sulfate and sodium hydroxide and any changes that may occur when excess sodium hydroxide was added. [2]

[Total: 5]

> **UNDERSTAND THESE TERMS**
>
> • precipitate
> • precipitation reaction
> • qualitative (analysis)
> • state symbols

22.2 Tests to identify common anions

1 A bottle containing a white solid is labelled only as 'Na salt of Group 7'.

Assuming that the Na part of the label is correct, how could you work out what the Group 7 part of the solid's identity was?

2 Figure 22.1 shows the label on a glass beaker containing a colourless solution. The writing on the label is smudged and could read either Na_2SO_4 or Na_2SO_3.

How could you use chemical tests to work out the correct identity of the solution in the beaker?

3 Some rocks and minerals contain carbonate ions which effervesce when hydrochloric acid is added to them.

  a Identify the gas given off when hydrochloric acid is added to substances containing carbonate ions. [1]

  b Describe how you would show it is the gas you identified in part a. You may use a labelled diagram in your answer. [2]

[Total: 3]

Figure 22.1: Smudged label

> **《 RECALL AND CONNECT 1 《**
>
> Write a balanced symbol equation for the reaction between calcium carbonate and hydrochloric acid. How can we use a top pan balance to measure the rate of this reaction? You may use a labelled diagram in your answer.

22.3 Tests to identify common gases

1   Using the information below, draw a table and match each gas to the test used
    to identify it and to the description of a positive result for that test.

Gas	Test	Positive result
ammonia (NH_3)	The gas is bubbled through limewater	relights.
carbon dioxide (CO_2)	Damp red litmus paper held in the gas	bleaches white.
chlorine (Cl_2)	A lit splint is held in the gas	which ignites with a squeaky pop.
hydrogen (H_2)	Damp litmus paper held in the gas	which is decolourised (turns purple to colourless).
oxygen (O_2)	The gas is bubbled through a solution of acidified potassium manganate(VII)	turns blue.
sulfur dioxide (SO_2)	A glowing splint held in the gas	which turns from colourless to cloudy/milky.

2   Electrolysis of sodium chloride and sodium sulfate solutions releases
    hydrogen at the cathode and chlorine or oxygen at the anode.

    Describe the tests you would do to confirm the identities of the
    gases released.   **[Total: 4]**

« RECALL AND CONNECT 2 «

How could you use the tests in these three sections to confirm the three
compounds present in NPK fertilisers? You do not need to describe how
you would test for the phosphate ion in your answer.

22.4 Quantitative analysis: acid-base titrations

1 The following instructions describe how to carry out an acid-base titration between sodium hydroxide and hydrochloric acid and using methyl orange as the indicator. These instructions are given in the wrong order.
What is the correct order?

A Fill the burette with hydrochloric acid. Read and record the initial volume on the burette.

B Read and record the final volume on the burette. This is the trial titre.

C Add a few drops of methyl orange indicator. The solution should be yellow.

D Continue to repeat the titrations until three results are within ±0.1 cm³ of each other.

E Run hydrochloric acid from the burette into the solution in the conical flask, swirling constantly, until the methyl orange indicator just changes to pale orange.

F Measure 25 cm³ of sodium hydroxide into the conical flask using a volumetric pipette and filler.

G Empty the burette and refill with sodium hyroxide solution from stock.

H Repeat the titration.

I Place the conical flask on a white tile beneath the burette.

2 **a** How is the volume of solution added from the burette calculated?

b Why is the volume measured in the first titration never used in calculations from the results?

c Name another indicator that could be used for this titration. What is the colour change you would see at the endpoint using this indicator?

3 Calcium hydroxide does not completely dissolve in water.

Calcium hydroxide is a base and reacts with hydrochloric acid.
The equation for the reaction is:

$$Ca(OH)_2 + 2HCl \rightarrow CaCl_2 + 2H_2O$$

To find its concentration, 20 cm³ portions of a saturated calcium hydroxide solution were titrated with 0.05 mol/dm³ hydrochloric acid.

The results are given in Table 22.1:

	Trial	Titre 1	Titre 2	Titre 3	Titre 4
Start volume (/cm³)	0.10	19.30	0.20	18.80	0.10
End volume (/cm³)	19.30	38.10	18.80	37.30	18.60
Titre (cm³)	19.20				

Table 22.1

a Copy and complete the table by calculating the volume of hydrochloric acid added for each titre. [2]

b Calculate the mean titre of hydrochloric added. [2]

c Calculate the number of moles of HCl in the mean titre. [2]

d How many moles of calcium hydroxide are in the 20.0 cm^3 of the solution? [2]

e Calculate the concentration of the calcium hydroxide solution in mol/dm^3. [2]

[Total: 10]

> **UNDERSTAND THESE TERMS**
>
> - acid-base titration
> - indicator
> - quantitative (analysis)
> - titre

REFLECTION

The reactions involved in this chapter have been linked back to three different contexts you have learned about in your course. Think or look back over your course to find any other points where they might be relevant. Make a list.

One place to check back to is the section on Electrolysis in Chapter 6. How can you make your notes here more comprehensive so that you know how to confirm the products formed at the electrodes from the electrolysis of different electrolytes?

SELF-ASSESSMENT CHECKLIST

Let's revisit the Knowledge focus and Exam skills focus for this chapter.

Decide how confident you are with each statement.

Now I can:	Show it	Needs more work	Almost there	Confident to move on
describe how characteristic colours produced by flame tests can be used to identify metal cations	Make flashcards with the flame colour on one side and the metal ion on the other. Quiz yourself with your friends and/or family or create a mind map.			
explore how precipitation reactions with solutions of sodium hydroxide and ammonia can be used to identify aqueous cations	Make flashcards for the cation tests and learn them in the same way as the flame tests.			

CONTINUED

Now I can:	Show it	Needs more work	Almost there	Confident to move on
discover how chemical analysis is used to determine the presence of anions	Make flashcards for the anion tests and learn them in the same way as the flame tests.			
develop simple practical techniques for proving the identity of different gases	Make flashcards for the gas tests and learn them in the same way as the flame tests.			
describe acid–base titration as a form of quantitative analysis	Write the steps for acid-base titrations onto separate cards, shuffle them and then rearrange them to put the steps in the correct order.			
describe how to identify the end-point of a titration using an indicator	Draw four diagrams showing a burette and conical flask underneath. Colour them in using different colours for before and after the end point with methyl orange and thymolphthalein indicators. When arranging your titration steps in order, place these diagrams next to the appropriate instruction.			
understand the 'calculate' command word and can answer 'calculate' questions.	When you are working on the 'calculate' questions, think about the places where you sometimes make mistakes when doing calculations. Make yourself a 'warning' list to remind you to check for that mistake. For example, a common mistake is forgetting to change cm^3 to dm^3 in concentration calculations.			

Exam practice 6

This section contains past paper questions from previous Cambridge exams, which draw together your knowledge on a range of topics that you have covered up to this point. These questions give you the opportunity to test your knowledge and understanding. Additional past paper practice questions can be found in the accompanying digital material.

The following question has an example student response and commentary provided. Once you have worked through the question, read the student response and commentary. Are your answers different to the sample answers?

1 a Alkanes and alkenes are both hydrocarbons.

    i How does the structure of alkenes differ from the structure of alkanes? [1]

    ii Is the straight-chain hydrocarbon $C_{22}H_{44}$ an alkane or an alkene? Explain your choice. [2]

    iii Describe how you could distinguish between pentane and pentene.

    test:

    result with pentane:

    result with pentene: [3]

[Total: 6]

Cambridge IGCSE Chemistry (0620) Paper 33 Q7a June 2015

Example student response	Commentary
1 a i Alkenes have a double bond between two carbons.	Correct answer. *This answer is awarded 1 out of 1 mark.*
ii It is an alkene.	The student identified the type of hydrocarbon correctly but has not explained their answer. Giving the general formula for alkenes would have completed the answer. *This answer is awarded 1 out of 2 marks.*
iii test: use bromine result with pentane: colour change result with pentene: colour change	Correct test. The result with pentane is incorrect and too vague for pentene. The colour of bromine before and after should be given for each result. *This answer is awarded 1 out of 3 marks.*

Now attempt the following similar question.

2 **a** A carboxylic acid and an ester are structural isomers.

    i State the meaning of the term *structural isomers*.   [2]

    ii Draw the structures of the carboxylic acid and the ester which both contain two carbon atoms.

        Show all of the atoms and all of the bonds.

        Name the carboxylic acid and the ester.   [4]

[Total: 6]

Cambridge IGCSE Chemistry (0620) Paper 43, Q6a November 2020

The following question has an example student response and commentary provided.

Work through the question first, then compare your answer to the sample answer and commentary. Do you feel that you need to improve your understanding of this topic?

3 Small amounts of carboxylic acids are also present in rainwater.

The structure of tartaric acid is shown.

    a On the structure draw a circle around one alcohol functional group.   [1]

    b Deduce the formula of tartaric acid to show the number of carbon, hydrogen and oxygen atoms.   [1]

[Total: 2]

Cambridge IGCSE Chemistry (0620) Paper 31, Q2c November 2021

Example student response	Commentary
3 **a** 	The student put a circle around the OH of a carboxylic acid (COOH) group and so has incorrectly identified the alcohol. *This answer is awarded 0 out of 1 mark.*
b $HOOC(CHOH)_2COOH$	The student has given a structural formula rather than the ratio of carbon, hydrogen and oxygen in the molecule. *This answer is awarded 0 out of 1 mark.*

Recognising functional groups in a molecule is critical in organic chemistry, as you saw in the commentary of the previous question. It is important to focus on the key characteristics of the functional group in each of the homologous series.

Now attempt the following question. Use the previous commentaries to support you as you answer.

4 The table shows the structures of some organic compounds.

compound	structure of compound	homologous series
G	H—C—C—C—O—H (with H, H, O and H atoms as shown)	carboxylic acid
H	H—C—C=C (with H atoms as shown)	
J	H—C—C—H (with H atoms as shown)	

a   Complete the table by naming the homologous series.

   The first one has been done for you. [2]

b   Draw the structure of a compound containing two carbon atoms which belongs to the same homologous series as compound H.

   Show all of the atoms and all of the bonds. [1]

c   State which compound in the table is an unsaturated hydrocarbon.

   Explain your answer. [1]

d   State which compound in the table reacts with aqueous sodium hydroxide.

   Explain your answer. [1]

e   State the names of the **two** compounds formed during the complete combustion of compound **J**. [2]

[Total: 7]

Cambridge IGCSE Chemistry (0620) Paper 31, Q5a–e November 2021

The following three questions have an example student response and commentary provided. Work through the question first, then compare your answer to the sample answer and commentary. How do your answers compare?

5 **a** Poly(ethene) is produced by combining many ethene molecules.

    i Name the general term used to describe the small molecules which combine to form a polymer. [1]

    ii Nylon is a polymer.

    State **one** use for nylon. [1]

    iii Describe **one** pollution problem caused by non-biodegradable plastics. [1]

                                        [Total: 3]

Cambridge IGCSE Chemistry (0620) Paper 31, Q5e November 2020

b But-2-ene forms a polymer.

    Suggest the name of the polymer formed from but-2-ene. **[Total: 1]**

Cambridge IGCSE Chemistry (0620) Paper 41, Q5c iv, November 2021

c **a** Part of a polyester chain is shown. This polyester is made from one monomer.

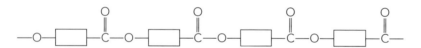

    i **On the diagram** draw a ring around one unit of the polymer that is repeated. [1]

    ii Name the type of polymerisation that produces polyesters. [1]

    iii Complete the diagram to show the structure of the monomer used to produce this polyester.

    Show all of the atoms and all of the bonds in the functional groups.

                                            [2]

b A polyamide is made from the two monomers shown.

    Complete the diagram to show a section of the polyamide made from the two monomers.

    Show all of the atoms and all of the bonds in the linkages.

                                            [2]

c   Naturally occurring polyamides are constituents of food.

   i   State the name given to naturally occurring polyamides.   [1]

   ii   Name the monomers which form naturally occurring polyamides.   [1]

[Total: 8]

Cambridge IGCSE Chemistry (0620) Paper 43 Q6b, c, d November 2020

Example student response	Commentary
5 a i monomer	Correct. Appropriate key term named. ***This answer is awarded 1 out of 1 mark.***
ii plastic coverings	Answer is not specific enough, too vague. A specific use must be named, e.g. rope, fishing nets, shirts or gearwheels. ***This answer is awarded 0 out of 1 mark.***
iii plastics take a long time to disappear.	Answer is not precise enough. While it is true that non-biodegradable plastics take a long time to disappear, a credit-worthy answer here would describe why this fact is a problem in the environment. ***This answer is awarded 0 out of 1 mark.***
b poly(but-2-ene)	Correct. Prefixing the name of the monomer with 'poly' is the usual way to name addition polymers. ***This answer is awarded 1 out of 1 mark.***
c a i	The student has identified the ester link in the polymer, rather than the repeat unit as asked for in the question. Identifying the ester link is also a common question to be asked, so it is important to read questions carefully and notice specifically what is wanted in the question. ***This answer is awarded 0 out of 1 mark.***
ii addition	Incorrect. Confusion about identifying the type of polymerisation present when given a section of chain can be cleared up by looking at the main backbone. If there are only C atoms in it, it is addition; if it contains O or N atoms, it is condensation. ***This answer is awarded 0 out of 1 mark.***
iii	The student has shown two carboxylic acid functional groups on the molecule where only one is relevant in the monomer used to make the polymer given in the question. A second functional group needs to be identified in place of one of the acid groups. ***This answer is awarded 1 out of 2 marks.***

Example student response	Commentary
b	The student has drawn the peptide link out correctly at two points in this section of polymer. However, the two monomers in the question had the same functional group at each end. The polymer as drawn here, would be made from monomers containing both functional groups. *This answer is awarded 1 out of 2 marks.*
c i proteins	Correct. Appropriate key term named. *This answer is awarded 1 out of 1 mark.*
ii amino acids	Correct. Appropriate key term named. *This answer is awarded 1 out of 1 mark.*

Now write an improved answer to Question 5 in the places where you lost marks.
Use the commentary to help you.

The following question has an example student response and commentary provided.

Work through the question first, then compare your answer to the sample answer and commentary. Did you make the same mistakes?

6   Lavandulol is a compound found in lavender flowers.
     The structure of lavandulol is shown.

a   On the diagram, draw a circle around the alcohol functional group.   [1]

b   How many carbon atoms are there in **one** molecule of lavandulol?   [1]

c   i   What feature of the lavandulol structure shows that it is unsaturated?   [1]

     ii   Describe a test to show that lavandulol is unsaturated.   [2]

          test:

          result:

d   Lavandulol can be extracted from lavender flowers.
     The following statements are about the procedure for extracting lavandulol.

     A   Stir the mixture and leave it for a few hours.

     B   Filter off the solid from the solution.

     C   Distil the solution.

     D   Add solvent to the ground up lavender flowers.

     E   Grind up the lavender flowers.

Put the statements A, B, C, D and E in the correct order.
The first one has been done for you. [2]

e Three different dye mixtures, **P**, **Q** and **R**, were placed on a sheet of
   chromatography paper. Two pure dyes, **X** and **Y**, were also placed on the
   same piece of chromatography paper. The experiment was carried out
   and the results are shown

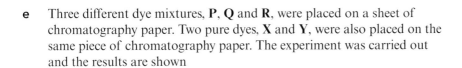

   i Where were the dyes placed on the chromatography paper at the
      start of the experiment? [1]

   ii Which dye mixture contained the greatest number of dyes? [1]

   iii Which dye mixture contained both dye **X** and dye **Y**? [1]

   [Total: 10]

Cambridge IGCSE Chemistry (0620) Paper 32, Q5 a, b, c, d, f March 2017

Example student response	Commentary
6 **a** CH₃, H, CH₂—(O—H); C=C—CH₂—C—H; CH₃, C—CH₃, CH₂	The response showed a good knowledge recall and application skills in being able to identify the functional group of alcohol. *This answer is awarded 1 out of 1 mark.*
b 10	This is a rather straightforward question that tests the ability to examine a diagram and identify the number of carbon atoms by looking at the diagram without any memory or knowledge recall. *This answer is awarded 1 out of 1 mark.*
c **i** double bond	The response here showed a good knowledge recall of the differences between unsaturated and saturated compounds. However, the student should be encouraged to be more specific in their answer by indicating the elements that are bonded together. This is because there are some functional groups with a double bond as well, but doesn't necessarily indicate an unsaturated compound. *This answer is awarded 1 out of 1 mark.*

Example student response	Commentary
ii bromine remains the same	The first response here on the test for saturation is correct. However, the results indicated by the student showed that the student was not able to recall if the results indicated were for saturated or unsaturated. ***This answer is awarded 1 out of 2 marks.***
d D, B, C, A	The student's response here showed a slight lack of understanding in how solvent extraction is done. Even though the student was able to get the second step correct by linking keywords such as 'grind' from the first step with 'ground' from the second step, the student missed the important next step of leaving the mixture to sit for a few hours. The student has made the commonly seen mistake of choosing to place 'leave it for a few hours' as the final step. ***This answer is awarded 0 out of 2 marks.***
e i solvent front	The student's response here showed a knowledge recall of terms used in chromatography, however, the student has mistaken this term for the starting line instead of the finishing line. ***This answer is awarded 0 out of 1 mark.***
ii Q	Here, the student's response displayed good examining skills in interpreting the results shown on the diagram and identify the correct dye mixture with the greatest number of dyes. ***This answer is awarded 1 out of 1 mark.***
iii Q	Here, the student's response again displayed good examining skills in being able to interpret the results shown on the diagram and identify the correct dye mixture which contained dye X and dye Y. ***This answer is awarded 1 out of 1 mark.***

Now that you've gone through the commentary, try to write an improved answer for the parts of Question 6 where you lost marks.

The following question has an example student response and commentary provided. Work through the question first, then compare your answer to the sample answer and commentary. How do they differ?

7   Concentrated ammonia solution gives off ammonia gas. Concentrated hydrochloric acid gives off hydrogen chloride gas. Ammonia, NH_3, and hydrogen chloride, HCl, are both colourless gases. Ammonia reacts with hydrogen chloride to make the white solid ammonium chloride.

Apparatus is set up as shown.

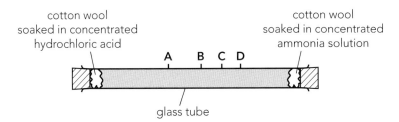

After ten minutes a white solid forms in the tube where the gases meet.

Some of the white solid is removed from the tube and dissolved in water.

Describe how the white solid could be tested to show it contains:

a   ammonium ions

test:

result: [3]

b   chloride ions.

test:

result: [3]

[Total: 6]

Cambridge IGCSE Chemistry (0620) Paper 43 Q6b June 2016

Example student response	Commentary
7 a Dissolve the solid in water and add litmus paper. The solution will turn blue.	The student has shown some awareness of how to carry out the test, but the details given are vague and lack clarity and precision. Recognising the need to make a solution is correct, but the student has not specified that sodium hydroxide needs to be added and the solution warmed to liberate ammonia gas. The use of litmus paper is correct to test the gas given off and the colour change to blue is also correct, but it is the litmus paper that turns blue, not the solution.
	This answer is awarded 0 out of 3 marks
b Add silver nitrate and hydrochloric acid. A white solid will be formed.	Using acidified silver nitrate will give a white precipitate in the presence of chloride so the student was mostly correct. However, hydrochloric acid contains chloride ions in solution and will give a positive result if used to acidify the silver nitrate, regardless of whether there are chloride ions present in the solid or not. Nitric acid needs to be used for this test.
	This answer is awarded 2 out of 3 marks

Analysis questions can often ask about a series of qualitative tests as in the previous question, or they can combine both qualitative and quantitative, as in the following question for you to try.

8   Dilute hydrochloric acid reacts with sodium carbonate solution.

$$2HCl\,(aq) + Na_2CO_3(aq) \rightarrow 2NaCl\,(aq) + H_2O(l) + CO_2(g)$$

a   Explain why effervescence is seen during the reaction.   [1]

b   Dilute hydrochloric acid was titrated with sodium carbonate solution.

   •   10.0 cm³ of 0.100 mol / dm³ hydrochloric acid were placed in a conical flask.

   •   A few drops of methyl orange indicator were added to the dilute hydrochloric acid.

   •   The mixture was titrated with sodium carbonate solution.

   •   16.2 cm³ of sodium carbonate solution were required to react completely with the acid.

   i   What colour would the methyl orange indicator be in the hydrochloric acid?   [1]

   ii   Calculate how many moles of hydrochloric acid were used.

                                          .... mol   [1]

   iii   Use your answer to **(b)(ii)** and the equation for the reaction to calculate the number of moles of sodium carbonate that reacted.

                                          .... mol   [1]

   iv   Use your answer to **(b)(iii)** to calculate the concentration of the sodium carbonate solution in mol / dm³.

                                          .... mol / dm³   [2]

                                                   [Total: 6]

Cambridge IGCSE Chemistry (0620) Paper 43, Q5a, b June 2016

> Acknowledgements

Cover Laguna Design/Getty Images